God,
A Word for Girls and Boys

God,
A Word for Girls and Boys

Jann Aldredge-Clanton

Illustrated by Pam Allen

GLAD RIVER PUBLICATIONS

Glad River Publications
P.O. Box 6356, Louisville, KY 40206-0356

Copyright © 1993 by Jann Aldredge-Clanton

All rights reserved. No part of this book may be reproduced, stored in a retrieval system, or transmitted, in any form or by any means, electronic, mechanical, photocopying, recording, or otherwise, without the written permission of Glad River Publications.

ISBN 0-9629898-3-5

Printed in the United States of America

Contents

INTRODUCTION	9
GETTING STARTED	
WHO IS GOD?	17
THE GREATEST LOVER (Luke 15:1–32)	19
GOD, OUR MOTHER (Deuteronomy 32:11–12)	22
OLD TESTAMENT STORIES AND SERMONS	
GOD, THE POTTER (Jeremiah 18:1–6)	25
GOD OF SURPRISES (Isaiah 55:8–9)	27
MIRIAM OF THE EXODUS (Exodus 2:1–10, 15:20–21; Micah 6:4)	28
A MAN WHO WOULD NOT COME DOWN (Nehemiah 6:1–16)	31
A WOMAN WHO LED HER COUNTRY TO FREEDOM (Judges 4 and 5)	32
HANGING ON FOR A BLESSING (Genesis 32:22–30)	35
RUTH, A FAITHFUL FRIEND (Ruth 1)	37
COMING ALIVE (Ezekiel 37:1–14)	40
A COURAGEOUS WOMAN (Esther 3–8)	41

JEALOUS BROTHERS (Genesis 37)	43
A BRAVE GIRL (2 Kings 5:1–14)	45
SLIME OR ROCK (1 Kings 18:20–40)	48
GROWING THROUGH SHARING (1 Kings 17:8–16)	49

NEW TESTAMENT STORIES AND SERMONS

THE PRODIGAL DAUGHTER (Luke 15:11–32)	53
A WOMAN WHO BUILT A CHURCH (Acts 16:11–15, 40)	55
EACH ONE IMPORTANT (1 Corinthians 12:12–27)	57
SWEET TARTS AND FAITH (Mark 9:14–24)	59
THREE KINDS OF SOIL (Matthew 13:3–9)	60
WHO GAVE THE MOST? (Luke 21:1–4)	62
FULL SACKS AND BARNS (Luke 12:16–21) [*appropriate near Halloween or Valentine's Day*]	64
SAYING "THANK YOU" TO GOD (Luke 17:11–19) [*appropriate near Thanksgiving Day*]	65
GOD COMES TO US (Romans 1:19–20; John 1:1–18) [*Advent*]	67
NO ROOM (Luke 2:1–7) [*Advent or Christmas*]	69
A NEW KIND OF LEADER (Matthew 21:1–11) [*Palm Sunday*]	71
MARY MAGDALENE AND BUTTERFLIES (John 20:1–18) [*Easter*]	72
BIRTHDAY GIFTS (Acts 2:1–21) [*Pentecost*]	75

OTHER STORIES OF FAITH AND COURAGE

A WOMAN WHO CHANGED OUR COUNTRY	77
LOVING THOSE WHO HURT US	80
THE DREAM IS ALIVE	83
ON MISSION FOR GOD	84

CONTENTS

BE SOMEBODY!	86
DREAM BIG!	88
A MISSIONARY DOCTOR	90
MOTHERS OF OUR FAITH [*appropriate for Mother's Day*]	92
WORKING TOGETHER	94
SOMETHING BETTER	96
WHAT YOU DON'T KNOW WILL HURT YOU	99
GLORIA'S BIG GOAL	101
A GIRL WHO WOULDN'T GIVE UP	103
FEELING FORGIVEN	106
PAMELA PEACEMAKER	108
A BOY WHO CONQUERED FEAR	110
DOING THE IMPOSSIBLE	112
HELP COMES [*Advent*]	115
CHRISTMAS GOES ON [*Christmastide*]	117

PRAYERS FOR ALL FEELINGS

WHEN WE FEEL AFRAID	121
WHEN WE FEEL LONELY	122
WHEN WE FEEL THANKFUL	122
WHEN WE FEEL ANGRY	124
WHEN WE FEEL SAD	126
WHEN WE FEEL HAPPY	127
WHEN WE FEEL GUILTY	129
WHEN WE'RE HAVING FUN	130

SONGS OF JOY

GOD IS	135
A PSALM OF UNITY	138
CHILD IN THE MANGER	139
MIRIAM'S TAMBOURINE	140
OUR GOD IS A SHE AND A HE	141
GOD IS LIKE NO OTHER	143
DEBORAH'S SONG	144
ALL CHILDREN TOGETHER	146
I AM SO GLAD	148
THERE IS ROOM IN MY HEART	150
PRAISE GOD ALL YOU LITTLE CHILDREN	151
INTO MY HEART	152
GOD'S BEAUTIFUL WORLD	153
DEEP AND WIDE	154
CLIMB SUNSHINE MOUNTAIN	155
WONDER SONG	156
NOTES	157
APPENDIX: INCLUSIVE-LANGUAGE RESOURCES FOR ADULTS	159

INTRODUCTION

One of the most pressing issues the contemporary church faces is gender and racial equality. Many denominations now recognize the importance of inclusive language, and they are trying to make changes in traditional worship services. Excellent resources guide the way for adult worship and education (see the Appendix, pp. 159–160). But little help is available for leaders of children. We continue to give our children limited images of God and of themselves. These messages they receive at church hold great power to limit our children for the rest of their lives.

One couple tried to counteract this negative influence their church was having on their three-year-old daughter. Over and over they told Rhonda how important she was to God and to them. They tried to give her an inclusive view of God and of people. They taught Rhonda to pray, "God is great. God is good. Let us thank God [not him] for this food." One day Rhonda and her mother were talking about God. Her mother referred to God as "she." Rhonda promptly corrected her, "No, Mommy, God is a he." Her mother replied, "God can be a she and a he." Rhonda insisted, "No, Mommy, that's not right. God is a he. God is a word for boys."

The masculine language of the church takes literal root in our children. They cannot grasp a theology of God as transcendent Spirit if they hear trusted authority figures in the church constantly calling God "he," "Father," "King." And they cannot develop a theology of male and female created equally in God's image if all they hear at church is "brothers," "sons," "men of

God." They cannot believe that Jesus loves girls and boys equally and calls both to be disciples if all they see in their Bible story books and denominational literature are illustrations of boys and men. Even the most adamantly liberated parents cannot counteract the powerful influence of these exclusive messages our children receive at church. No matter how much we may want children to develop an inclusive theology, if we as church do not change the verbal and visual images we use in teaching children, they will come to believe that "God" is a word for boys.

Out of a profound conviction that children need to feel that God is a word for girls as well as boys, we have developed these resources for those working with children. This book provides inclusive materials for the religious education of children in the church and in the home. Illustrations and language are inclusive in gender and race. The stories, pictures, songs, prayers, and activities in this collection will help teachers and parents instill in children the theological truth that all are created equally in God's image. Through a balance of masculine, feminine, and non-gender-specific pictures and references to God, the resources in this book teach that God includes and transcends female and male. All language for people is inclusive as well. Stories highlight girls as well as boys, female as well as male role models of different races. Biblical examples include as many women as men. These materials tell and show children that God is for girls as much as for boys and that God is for children of all races. The hope is that this truth will become deeply ingrained in the minds and emotions of children.

A little girl's letter to God underscores this need to teach children that God transcends masculine gender: "Dear God, are boys better than girls? I know you are one but try to be fair."[1] This little girl has internalized messages that church and society value males more than females. Feeling put down, she appeals to the highest authority she knows. She has been taught that God is loving and just, but male. Thus she feels the cards are stacked against her. She wonders if God can be truly fair. How can a "he" God believe girls are as good as boys?

My experiences of ministry with abused children have also deepened my conviction that the church must change its God-language. Two little girls with a history of sexual abuse illustrate the problem. Because their father sexually abused them, the eleven-year-old girl and her nine-year-old sister were placed in a foster home. When the social worker learned that their foster father was also abusing them, she placed them in the home of their grandparents. The grandfather also sexually abused them. For these girls the traditional image of God as father carries nothing but negative connotations. For this reason they did not like coming to church. Other children who come to our churches have no father in the home; some of these fathers never contact their children. If we use the father image to teach these children about God, they will grow up feeling that God is abusive or absent.

By using language for God other than masculine, the stories and songs and prayers in this book help these children get beyond any negative experience of fathers in order to feel the nurturing, tender care of God. Jesus said that "whoever causes one of these little ones who believe in me to sin" would be better off having a great stone round their necks and drowned in the sea (Matt. 18:6). Masculine God-language hinders many children from establishing relationships of trust with God. In addition, calling God "he" causes boys to commit the sin of arrogance. They grow up believing boys are better than girls because they learn that "God is a boy." Calling the supreme power of the universe "he" causes girls to commit the sin of devaluing themselves. For the sake of "these little ones," we must change the way we talk about God and about human beings.

In our patriarchal society, the devaluation of non-Caucasian races parallels that of women. Basic to patriarchy is a hierarchical structure with white males on top. All others are marginalized and characterized as deviant from the norm of the white male. Language has served as a powerful support of this system, which oppresses non-Caucasians as well as women. Martin Luther King, Jr., underscores the power of language in the development of children's self-concepts:

> In Roget's Thesaurus there are some 120 synonyms for "blackness" and at least 60 of them are offensive — such words as "blot," "soot," "grime," "devil," and "foul." There

are some 134 synonyms for "whiteness," and all are favorable, expressed in such words as "purity," "cleanliness," "chastity," and "innocence." A white lie is better than a black lie. The most degenerate member of a family is the "black sheep," not the "white sheep." Maybe the English language should be "reconstructed" so that teachers will not be forced to teach Negro children 60 ways to despise themselves and thereby perpetuate this false sense of inferiority and white children 134 ways to adore themselves and thereby perpetuate this false sense of superiority.[2]

Churches have contributed to the low self-esteem of black children by teaching them to sing such lines as these:

> Now wash me, and I shall be whiter than snow.

and

> Who's that dressed in white?
> It must be the children of the Israelites.
> Who's that dressed in black?
> It must be the hypocrites turning back.

Before the age of eleven or twelve, certain types of abstract thinking remain beyond children. From age eleven or twelve onward, thinking becomes more abstract. Younger children cannot reason about abstract concepts like existence, truth, justice, and God. They tend to leap to conclusions too quickly.[3] Thus when we call God "he," they conclude that God is a male. When the only pictures they see of God and Jesus are white, they conclude that God is white. Most children do not show a well-developed abstract understanding of the appearance-reality distinction until about age eleven or twelve.[4] If all our pictures of God are masculine and white but we say that God is not really a white man, children cannot grasp this distinction between appearance and reality. If all our pictures of Christ's disciples are white males, it will be difficult for children to understand that females and nonwhites can really be followers of Christ. Distinguishing false from true belief involves even more abstract thinking than distinguishing between appearance and reality.[5] Thus children under the age of eleven or twelve do not question what teachers and parents say about God. They accept everything as literal truth.

At an early age, boys and girls learn to imagine a masculine God. Psychologist David Heller asked nine-year-old Arthur how he would feel if God were the opposite sex. Arthur adamantly responded, "God is a man, for sure. I couldn't even imagine God being a lady. No, sir. Boy, that would change the world." In spite of his obvious discomfort over the prospect of a female God, Arthur recognized the profound effects of the way we imagine God. Twelve-year-old Tamara, old enough to question traditional images of God, prophesied as to how a female God would "change the world." She said that if God were a woman, "there would be less violence in the world." Eleven-year-old Becky Sue said that she saw no good reason why a girl couldn't be God "or at least president of a country."[6]

The way children conceive God affects and reflects the way they feel about themselves. Becky Sue's response indicates that the possibility of a female God opens new opportunities for her and for other girls. If God were female, then maybe a girl could be president of a country. The deity serves as a kind of role model, an image to strive toward. If all our images for God are masculine, then girls feel ambivalent about striving toward this ideal.

Children's concepts of God reflect sex-role socialization. The boys in David Heller's study described a rational, pragmatic, active, and aloof God. The girls described a more aesthetic, artistic, passive, and intimate God. The boys reflected a technological and rational rather than a feeling-oriented approach to the sacred. However, the boys had a hard time understanding how a God who is actively involved in their lives can at the same time remain so aloof. The boys implied a need for greater closeness to God. The girls indicated an interest in the mystery of partnership with the deity. The God of the girls is more intimacy-oriented than power-oriented. The socialization process of girls and boys thus finds its way into their concepts of God.[7]

Exclusively masculine images of God present problems for boys and girls. Boys have trouble developing personal, intimate relationships with a masculine God, whom they view as aloof. Girls lack a powerful role model if God is masculine. Gender-inclusive language for God will give children a more balanced view of God and of themselves. They can then conceive of God as intimate, as well as active; artistic, as well as pragmatic; emotional, as well as rational; powerful, as well as gentle. Developing an androgynous concept of God will help children to claim their own androgyny. As children reach a more wholistic understanding of God and of themselves, they will come closer to the truth of God and to health for themselves. They will develop more fully their potential as human beings in the image of God (Gen. 1:27).

Children now learn to use gender-inclusive language in school. For over twenty years the generic "he," "man," and "mankind" have been passing out of standard English usage. Textbook publishers and professional journals in the behavioral sciences require inclusive language. The National Council of Teachers of English recommends avoiding generic pronouns "to avoid the impression that every person is a 'he.' "[8] Children are no longer learning that "he" and "man" can mean masculine or feminine. If children continue to hear exclusively masculine language only at church, they will draw one of two conclusions: (1) Since females are included everywhere except in church, God must be partial to males, and the church's message and mission are limited to males; (2) the church is hopelessly archaic and irrelevant.

The future of children and of the church depends upon our willingness to change the traditional language of the church to eliminate gender and racial bias. Our concern for the church and for children has led us to write these inclusive-language resources for children. Vital to the church is the instilling of inclusive images within our children. Even the most progressive adults will testify that it is hard for them to get beyond masculine images of God because they were so deeply embedded within their subconscious minds when they were children. If an inclusive theology of God informs the earliest religious education of children, then the church will not only survive but will flourish as a community of reconciliation, justice, and peace.

These stories, pictures, songs, prayers, and other resources for teaching children apply a theology of inclusiveness to concrete experiences of children. They have emerged out of our ministry with children. We have used these materials with children and have had good response. The resources target elementary children in general with the confidence that teachers can adapt them to various grade levels.

The resources in this book can be used in Sunday School classes, in Bible school classes, in day-care centers, in separate services for children (children's church), or as part of regular Sunday morning worship services. Given prominence in worship services, they can be powerful teaching tools for children and adults alike. Focusing on children in a worship service gives them a feeling of being a vital part of the church community. The children's sermon thus becomes a "teachable moment" with great potential for permanent influence on thought and behavior. Adults can often relate to the concrete object lesson or story format of a children's sermon even better than to the more abstract "adult" sermon. Whether used in children's church or in "big church," these resources can bring new life to worship. Inclusion of children and children's songs and stories in adult worship services provides a valuable intergenerational experience. While teaching our children, we learn about the spiritual life from them. The prophet Isaiah said, "a little child shall lead them" (11:6b), and Christ said, "unless you turn and become like children, you will never enter the kingdom of heaven" (Matt. 18:2).

Parents, grandparents, and other care-givers can also use this collection with children in the home. It can serve as a bedtime storybook, a resource for family devotions, and a songbook for family gatherings.

This collection comes to you as an invitation to join in the adventure of creating inclusive resources for children, to come alive to your own creativity and the creativity of the children with whom you live and work, to join with the childlike, creative Spirit in "making all things new" (Rev. 21:5).

GETTING STARTED

WHO IS GOD?

Who is God? [*Give time for the children to respond.*] This is a difficult question. No one has all the answers to this question. God is so much more than what we can think or imagine or put into words.

The Bible helps us to understand something about God by giving us metaphors for God. A metaphor is a picture in words. A metaphor helps us to understand something very difficult by comparing it to something we know. The Bible uses many metaphors for God. These metaphors for God show us what God is like.

The Bible tells us that God is like a shepherd because God takes care of us as a shepherd takes care of sheep (Ps. 23, John 10:11–15). The Bible pictures God as a fortress, a shield, a strong tower, and a shelter, because God protects us, just as all of these things protect people from danger (Ps. 91:2–4, 61:3). The Bible says that Jesus is like a vine, and we are like branches connected to this vine, because when we believe in Jesus we become like Jesus (John 15:1–5). God is the beginning and the end of everything that exists (Rev. 1:8). Jesus is like a door to the best life here on earth and after we die (John 10:9). God is like a father who tenderly takes care of his children (Ps. 103:13). God is like a mother who comforts her children (Isa. 66:13). God is like a woman who is hurting while she gives birth, because God hurts for her children (Isa. 42:14). God is like all these, but so much more. [*Show the picture on page 18 and invite the children to point out metaphors for God.*]

GETTING STARTED — 19

The Bible also says that God is like a lily or rose, a light, bread, a dove, a rock. [*Show these objects. Give time for the children to respond to the following questions. Encourage them to think about these metaphors.*]

How do you think God is like a lily or rose? (Song of Solomon 2:1)
How is God like light? (Ps. 27:1; John 8:12)
The Bible says that Jesus is the Bread of Life. How is Jesus like bread? (John 6:35)
How is God like a dove? (Matt. 3:16)
How is God like a rock? (Ps. 71:3)

God is so much more than any words we have to describe God. These metaphors, or word-pictures, help us to know God.

Prayer

Dear God, we thank you for giving us minds to learn about you, words to help us talk about you, and feelings to help us know you. May we always be open to learn more about you and to know you better. Amen.

Activity Center

On tables place rocks, slices of bread, light bulbs, lilies, roses, branches, pictures of doves and of mothers and fathers. Also make available crayons, construction paper, used magazines, scissors, and paste. Ask the children to examine the objects and talk about what they show about God. Then ask them to draw or make collages to show how they picture God.

THE GREATEST LOVER
(Luke 15:1–32)[9]

Jesus told stories to help us understand more about God. These stories are called parables. Jesus told two short stories to help us understand how much God loves us.

There once was a woman who lost a coin. [*Hold up a silver dollar.*] She had ten coins and lost just one of them. We might think she wouldn't worry very much about losing just one coin, when she still had nine left. We might think she would look around for awhile, and then give up. But no! It was too valuable to her! This coin was so precious that the woman spent a long time looking for it. She moved all her furniture, swept out the whole house, searched and searched and searched until she finally found it. When she found it, she was so happy that she rushed next door to tell her friends.

Jesus told another story about a little lost sheep. [*Show a picture of a sheep.*] The shepherd who took care of this sheep had ninety-nine other sheep, but he missed this one lost sheep. Surely he could do without this one little sheep if he had ninety-nine others. But no! This sheep was too important to him. So the shepherd left the others for a while to go and search for the lost sheep. When he found it, he was so happy that he told all his friends and neighbors. And they celebrated together.

In these stories Jesus shows us what God is like. God is the greatest lover of all. God is like the woman looking for her one lost coin. God thinks we are precious, just like the woman thought the coin was too precious to lose. God is also like the shepherd searching for one lost sheep. When we go away from God, God goes to find us. No matter how many people there are in the world, God thinks each one of us is important. God loves us enough to want us to be the very best we can be. There is nothing we could do that would ever make God stop loving us. God longs for us to be all we can be. We can be the best when we trust God to help us and follow God's way. God is the greatest lover of all.

Prayer

God, our greatest Lover, thank you for showing us how much you love us. We're so glad that you love us even when we go away from you. Help us to stay close to you so we can be all you created us to be. We want to love you too. Amen.

Activity Center

Construct a gold-colored box. (A cardboard box can be covered with gold wrapping paper, or a wooden box can be painted gold. The color gold represents the value of the contents of the box.) Cover the bottom of the box with green felt to represent grass. Cut strips of blue felt for water, black felt for rocks, and strips of brown felt for the sheepfold. Make cardboard sheep figures and a cardboard figure of the shepherd. In another gold box place brown felt to represent the floor of a house. Cut strips of various colors to represent the furniture. Place in the box a cardboard figure of a woman and ten coins (which can be play money). Let the children play with the boxes, reaching down into them to move the figures or taking the materials out of the boxes. Encourage them to tell the parables or create new stories. Then ask the children to draw or paint the parables using colored pencils, water colors, or magic markers. Give the children time to talk about their creations.[10]

GOD, OUR MOTHER
(Deuteronomy 32:11–12)

God is so much more than we can ever imagine. It's hard to picture God in our minds because God is so much greater than anything or anyone we've ever seen. But the Bible helps us to imagine God by painting many different word-pictures of God. These pictures help us to imagine God by showing us what God is like.

One of the pictures of God in the Bible is of a mother bird. [*Show the picture of the mother and baby eagles on page 23.*] God is like a mother eagle who teaches her young eagles to fly and to hunt their own food. When the little eagles are old enough to leave the nest, their mother shakes the nest and flutters her wings over them to get them out of the nest on their own. Then she takes them on her wings to teach them to fly. They get the feel of flying by riding along on her wings. Then when the mother thinks the young birds are ready, she swoops down to let them fly by themselves. You can imagine that this might be a little scary for them at first. Maybe you have had this feeling if you have learned to ride a bicycle. Your mother or father or older sister or brother ran along beside you helping you learn to balance. Then she let go, and you had to ride by yourself. You may have felt scared at first. So the young birds are probably a little shaky at first, when their mother lets go. And the mother bird has to trust them enough to let go of them. She has to believe that they can fly on their own. But the mother stays close by while they are learning to fly. She stays close enough to swoop under them and catch them if they are having trouble flying by themselves, or if they get too tired to continue flying on their own.

The Bible says that God is like a mother eagle and like human mothers. Like a mother, God wants you to grow up and to learn to take care of yourselves. And God wants to help you when you learn new things and when you feel weak and tired. God is like a loving, strong, and gentle mother who wants you to grow up to be all you can be. Like a mother, God loves you and wants the best for you.

GETTING STARTED ———————————————————— 23

Prayer

God, our Mother, we thank you that you love us so much to want the best for us. Thank you for trusting us enough to let us do things on our own. We thank you that you love us enough to let go of us so that we can learn new things. Stay near us and help us to become all that we can be. Amen.

Activity Center

Help the children make birds' nests with twigs and grass and leaves. Make birds out of bright-colored paper or cardboard. If possible, use the Japanese art of origami to make flapping-winged cranes. Make a larger bird to represent the mother and smaller birds to represent the young birds. Involve the children in acting out the mother bird's stirring up the nest to get the young birds out. Then ask the children to take a mother bird in one hand and a baby bird in the other hand to show how a young bird flies on its mother's wings, and then learns to fly on its own as the mother bird slowly drops down. Encourage the children to play with the birds, tell the story, or create new stories. What does a mother bird show us about God's love?

OLD TESTAMENT STORIES AND SERMONS

GOD, THE POTTER
(Jeremiah 18:1–6)

Does anyone know what a potter is? A potter is someone who makes flower pots and all kinds of pots and jars out of clay. [*Show the children several pieces of pottery.*] Now make anything you would like to make with your play dough. [*Take some play dough yourself and start trying to make a flower pot. Make a mess of it.*] Can anyone tell what this is that I'm trying to make? Well, it's supposed to be a flower pot, but I messed it up. The good thing about play dough is that we can easily correct our mistakes. We can even start all over again if we want to. That's what I'm going to do. I'm going to rework the play dough into a new flower pot. [*Make as good-looking a flower pot as possible!*] There! That's better! Still not perfect, but better. What have you made? [*Let the children tell what they have made.*] Did any of you make mistakes and start over?

The prophet Jeremiah told the people of Israel that God was not pleased with them because they had forgotten to worship and obey God. God had not made a mistake in making them, like I made a mistake in making the pot. But the people made mistakes. They disobeyed God. Jeremiah's good news was that they had another chance. God would forgive them and change them. God would make them brand new, just like I could make a new pot.

God is like a potter. God can mold and change us into new

people, just as a potter can shape clay into a new pot. You and I make mistakes. We do things that are wrong. And we don't always do the good things that we should do. But the good news is that God will forgive us and make us like new. Let's put ourselves into God's hands right now.

Prayer

God, we ask that you will forgive us and make us new. Mold us into what you want us to be. Amen.

Activity Center

On tables place clay pots that have pieces broken off. Help the children glue the pots back together. Also invite the children to make play dough pots of various sizes and shapes. Encourage them to start over if they make mistakes. Ask them to talk with you about ways God is like a potter. Show them the picture of the potter (page 26).

GOD OF SURPRISES
(Isaiah 55:8–9)

The Bible tells us that God's ways are not like our ways, and God's thoughts are not like our thoughts. God's thoughts and actions are much greater than our thoughts and actions. In fact, God's thoughts and actions are so much greater than ours that we could never have imagined some of the things God has created.

Have you ever been to a zoo? Did you see the giraffe with the long, skinny neck and the big round hippopotamus with the strange-looking face? Could you have ever thought up such funny animals to create? God must love to surprise us!

[*Hold up an avocado seed, and ask the children if they know what it is. Then show the avocado it grows into. Hold up a watermelon seed, and ask what it is. Then show a watermelon.*] Now suppose you had never seen these seeds and these fruits, and I asked you which seed would grow into a watermelon. What would you say? [*Hold up the avocado seed.*] I would think that this big seed would grow into this great big watermelon. [*Hold up the watermelon seed.*] And this little bitty seed would grow into this small avocado. But God made this tiny seed to grow into this big watermelon, and this bigger seed to grow into this small avocado. God must love surprises!

When we really look at the things all around us that God made, we are surprised. Look at this seed. [*Show the children an acorn.*] What do you think it will become? What it grows into cannot fit in this room, because it's too big. It grows into a huge oak tree. Who would ever guess that this tiny seed would grow into a huge oak tree? God's thoughts are surely greater than our thoughts. God, our great Mother who gave birth to the whole world, must love surprises!

Do you like surprises? I think we all do. Maybe that's why God created the world with so many surprises in it. God is constantly doing things we don't expect, that we couldn't even imagine. Start looking all around you for God's surprises.

Prayer

God, how glad we are that you made a world with so many fun, exciting surprises. May we always keep our eyes open to the surprises you create for us to enjoy. Amen.

Activity Center

On tables place various fruits and seeds. Ask the children to try to match the seeds with the fruits. Invite the children to talk about why they think God made so many different kinds of fruits and other things. Why is it hard to match some of the seeds and fruits?

MIRIAM OF THE EXODUS
(Exodus 2:1–10, 15:20–21; Micah 6:4)

What does "exodus" means? [*Give time for the children to respond.*] There was a very important Exodus recorded in the Bible. Who can tell us about that Exodus? [*Let the children tell a little of the story of the Israelites' leaving slavery in Egypt to go to freedom.*] Often we hear about Moses leading the people of Israel out of slavery in Egypt. But the Bible tells us that Moses was not the only leader. His sister Miriam and his brother Aaron also led the people out of slavery to freedom (Micah 6:4).

Miriam's part in the Exodus began when she was a little girl, probably around seven years old. The cruel king of Egypt became afraid of the people of Israel because they were growing in numbers. He feared they would become strong enough to escape from slavery and fight against Egypt. So the king, also called Pharaoh, forced them to do more work and harder work with little rest.

Pharaoh hoped that many would die from such hard work. But instead, the people of Israel continued to grow in numbers. So the cruel Pharaoh ordered that all the Israelite baby boys be killed. Miriam's mother had a baby boy. For three months she hid him from the king. When he got too big to hide in the house, she made a basket, put the baby in the basket, and floated the basket at the edge of the river. Miriam hid in the tall grass nearby to guard her baby brother. When the daughter of the cruel king came down to the river to bathe and saw the baby in the basket, Miriam had enough courage to ask her, "Shall I go and get you a nurse from the Hebrew women to nurse the child for you?" Pharaoh's daughter was kind enough to let the baby's own mother nurse him. Then Pharaoh's daughter took the boy as her son and named him Moses. Miriam played a big part in saving Moses' life so that he could grow up to be one of the leaders of the Exodus.

Miriam grew up to be an important leader of the Exodus herself. She was also a prophet of Israel. A prophet speaks and teaches the word of God. God used Miriam to lead her people out of slavery in Egypt. Her people left Egypt and came to the Sea of Reeds. The king of Egypt and his army followed close behind. Just when Miriam's people thought the Egyptians were going to catch them and destroy them, God parted the sea. The Israelites went across on dry land. The strong and courageous Miriam, along with Moses and Aaron, led the people across to safety. [*Show the picture on page 29.*]

Miriam wrote a song to praise God for this glorious deliverance. Miriam and all the women played tambourines and danced to this song of praise. The Song of Miriam is one of the oldest parts of the Bible. It begins like this: "Sing to God, for God has triumphed gloriously; the horse and rider God has thrown into the sea."

Prayer

Mighty God, we thank you for giving power to Miriam, Moses, and Aaron to lead the Israelites to freedom. We praise you for the miracle of the Exodus. Use us also to lead people to greater freedom. Amen.

Activity Center

On a table place materials for the children to make tambourines. Include paper plates, jingle bells one inch in diameter (which can be purchased inexpensively at a craft or hobby store), hot glue (purchased at a craft store), magic markers in bright colors, yarn (optional). Help the children make tambourines: (1) glue the paper plates back to back; (2) use bright-colored markers to make designs on the outside of the plates; (3) glue jingle bells around the edges of the plates. (Alternative method: string bells on yarn and glue the yarn to the edges of the plates. If you use this method, Elmer's Glue or rubber cement will work.) Lead the children in singing "Miriam's Tambourine" (on page 140) until they learn the words and tune. Then lead them in dancing around the room, playing their tambourines and singing "Miriam's Tambourine."

A MAN WHO WOULD NOT COME DOWN
(Nehemiah 6:1–16)

The Bible tells us about a man named Nehemiah, who was a high official in the court of King Artaxerxes of Persia. Nehemiah had great military, political, and administrative skill. Nehemiah had been living far away from his home in the land of Judah. When enemies had conquered Nehemiah's homeland, Nehemiah's family and many other people from his country had to leave. They went into exile in other countries.

After many years Nehemiah heard that conditions looked better in his homeland. The country was no longer at war. Nehemiah thought about the beautiful capital city of Jerusalem. During the war, the great walls around Jerusalem had been destroyed. Nehemiah believed that the walls should be rebuilt. He prayed for God to permit him to go to Jerusalem and help rebuild the wall of Jerusalem.

Nehemiah's prayer was answered. King Artaxerxes granted Nehemiah's request to go to Jerusalem, without asking a single question. Now Nehemiah was determined to rebuild the wall of Jerusalem. He knew that God had given him the important job of rebuilding the wall. He worked night and day. He led the work of rebuilding the wall. Nehemiah would not let anything get in the way of his doing what God wanted him to do. He kept on even when people made fun of him. He kept on even when the work seemed impossible. He kept on even when people tried to stop him.

When the wall was almost finished, some evil people plotted to get Nehemiah off track. Nehemiah was high up on the wall. His enemies tried to get him to come and meet with them. But he sent messengers back to tell them, "I am doing a great work and I cannot come down. I cannot leave the work and come down to meet with you." Four times his enemies sent messages asking him to come down and meet with them. And four times Nehemiah sent the message back that he would not come down! Because Nehemiah refused to be distracted from the work God had given him to do, he and his workers finally finished the wall. All the countries nearby recognized that this wall was the work of God. Even Nehemiah's enemies had to admit that the wall had been rebuilt with the help of God.

God has important jobs for each one of us. God wants us to do our best in these jobs. It's important to work hard and not let anything get us off track. God wants us to be determined, like Nehemiah, to finish the work God gives us to do.

Prayer

Thank you, God, for giving each of us special work to do. May we be determined to do our best and to finish the work you give us. Amen.

Activity Center

Scatter building blocks or large cardboard boxes on the floor. Let each child take a turn building a wall, while the others try to distract her or him and then try to knock the wall down. The child building the wall should keep working until the wall is complete. Have the children sit in a circle. Ask them to talk about their feelings when building the wall and when trying to distract the person building the wall. Play charades, with the children acting out some task that was hard to complete, but which they finished because they would not give up.

A WOMAN WHO LED HER COUNTRY TO FREEDOM
(Judges 4 and 5)

For twenty years the king of Canaan had treated the people of Israel cruelly. King Jabin had destroyed the land of the people of Israel and had made them serve as slaves. The people of Israel cried out to God for help.

OLD TESTAMENT ———————————————————— 33

God answered their prayers through a strong leader named Deborah. Deborah was a prophet: that is, she spoke the word of God to the people. She also served as a judge, settling the disputes of her people and telling them what to do. In these roles as prophet and judge, she held the highest power in the country. She was the top leader of Israel, like the president of a country today. God also gave her power to be the military leader who would save her people from the cruel King Jabin.

Deborah called for Barak, one of Israel's best military leaders. She asked Barak to gather ten thousand soldiers to fight King Jabin's army. Deborah let Barak know that she was not afraid of Sisera, leader of Jabin's army. And she was not afraid of his nine hundred chariots of iron. Deborah believed that God would help them gain freedom for the people of Israel. Barak felt inspired by

Deborah's faith in God and by her courage. He told Deborah that he would go fight Sisera and his army if she would go with him.

The soldiers of Israel were not as well-armed as those of Canaan. But Deborah's faith and courage led the Israelites forward into the battle. Deborah knew the exact time to strike. She said to Barak and the army, "Up! For this is the day God will lead us to victory!"

Because of Deborah's strong leadership and faith in God, the Israelites did win the victory. The Israelites would now enjoy freedom. To celebrate this great victory, Deborah wrote a song of praise to God. This Song of Deborah has become part of the Bible. It goes like this:

> That the leaders took the lead in Israel,
> that the people offered themselves willingly,
> bless God!
> Hear, O kings; give ear, O princes;
> to God I will sing,
> I will make melody to the God of Israel.
> Awake, awake, Deborah!
> Awake, awake, utter a song! (Judges 5:1–3, 12)

Deborah gave credit to God for giving her the strength and courage to save the people of Israel from the cruel King Jabin. This terrible king was destroying the Israelites until Deborah arose as "mother of Israel" (Judges 5:7). With God's help Deborah led her people to victory and freedom.

Prayer

God of power, we thank you for giving power to Deborah to lead the Israelites to freedom. Give us power and courage for the work you have for us to do. Amen.

Activity Center

Set up a flannel board (made of plywood covered with solid black or dark blue flannel cloth) in the activity center. On the board place figures (made of felt or flannel or paper with felt strips glued to the backs) to represent Deborah, Barak, Jael, Sisera, various people who come to Deborah for settlement of disputes, and soldiers. Invite the children to take turns telling the story of Deborah in her roles as judge, prophet, and military leader. Encourage the children to use their imaginations and tell stories of other adventures she may have had as the leader of Israel. Sing "Deborah's Song" (page 144).

HANGING ON FOR A BLESSING
(Genesis 32:22–30)

In the Bible we read about Jacob, who had the strange experience of wrestling with an angel. All night long Jacob wrestled with the angel. When it was almost morning, the angel saw that he could not win against Jacob. So the angel touched Jacob's thigh and put it out of joint. Jacob still would not give up, but kept wrestling with the angel. The angel said to Jacob, "Let me go, because it's almost morning." But Jacob said, "I will not let you go, unless you bless me." Jacob refused to let go of the angel until he received a blessing. So the angel blessed Jacob and gave him a new name. From then on his name would be Israel, and he would be the father of the nation of Israel. Jacob received a blessing by hanging on.

A modern-day person also received a blessing by hanging on. This person was named Cathy. She played the oboe, a woodwind instrument that looks much like a clarinet. But it has a delicate double reed that you blow to get the sound. The reed has to be just the right length and thickness to get the mellow sound the oboe is supposed to make. After Cathy had been playing the oboe just a year, she decided to play a solo in the state band contest. She knew that she was at a disadvantage because she had not been playing as long as most of the students who entered. But she liked a challenge, so she entered anyway. Months before the contest, Cathy started practicing the solo. She practiced every single day for hours and hours.

When the time came for the contest, Cathy knew that she would do well. She could play her solo perfectly from memory. And she had learned to get a beautiful, mellow tone, especially with her favorite reed that she had broken in so that it was just right. Several hours before she was to play her solo, she was warming up in a practice room. A student from another school barged in, hitting her arm with the door. This caused Cathy to knock her best reed against her teeth and break it. She was so upset! She didn't know what to do. Since she didn't have much time left before she had to perform, she quickly took one of her spare reeds and started trying to break it in. But the sound she got from it was not that good. She wanted to run and hide in a corner and cry. She had worked so hard on the solo, and now she couldn't make it sound right. But she went on and played the solo. The judges gave her a third place rating, instead of the first place she had wanted. Their main criticism was her tone. She had looked forward to earning a first place medal to wear on her band uniform. She went home that day feeling crushed. Some of her friends who had not worked so hard had won medals. It was just not fair! She felt mad at the student who made her break her best reed, mad at the reed for breaking, mad at herself for choosing to play such a delicate instrument as the oboe, mad at the sun for daring to shine after this had happened to her, and mad at God for letting this happen! She thought she deserved better.

After the contest, Cathy wanted to give up playing the oboe. After all, she might work as hard as she could and get shot down again. But with the encouragement of her parents and her band director, she continued to play the oboe. She decided to hang on and keep trying. She entered the contest the following year more determined than ever. She practiced harder than ever before. And this time she made sure that she had several reeds that were just right. That year Cathy earned the highest possible rating and received the medal she had been wanting.

But the first place rating and the medal were not the greatest and longest lasting of the blessings Cathy received. The main blessing was that she learned to hang on even when things get difficult. She learned that blessings come by hanging on, refusing to let go, and continuing to struggle.

You probably have never wrestled with an angel, as Jacob did. But you have probably had to struggle with something that was difficult, as Cathy did. Maybe everything was going wrong and you just wanted to quit. Remember that when you hang on and keep on struggling, a blessing will come. Something good will come.

Prayer

Dear God, you know that often we want the blessings without the struggle, the good things without any hard work. Help us to know that many good things come only from hanging on and struggling through hard times and hard work. May we learn from Jacob and from Cathy to hang on for a blessing. Amen.

Activity Center

On tables place drawing paper, magic markers, crayons, used magazines, scissors, and paste. Invite the children to draw pictures or make collages representing the stories of Jacob with the angel or of Cathy at the band contest. Also give the children the option of making a picture or writing a story about a personal experience of hanging on when things got hard.

RUTH, A FAITHFUL FRIEND
(Ruth 1)

How many of you have a good friend? [*Give time for the children to respond.*] Some of you may have a best friend. What makes someone a good friend? [*Let the children discuss the traits of a good friend.*]

The Bible gives us a picture of a good friend. Her name is Ruth. Ruth shows us how to be a good friend.

Ruth lived in a country called Moab. The country of Moab had food in a time when many of the countries close by had none. People came to Moab to escape the famine in their land. Naomi and her husband Elimelech came from Bethlehem to find food in Moab. Naomi and Elimelech had two sons named Mahlon and Chilion. Ruth, a Moabite woman, and Mahlon fell in love and

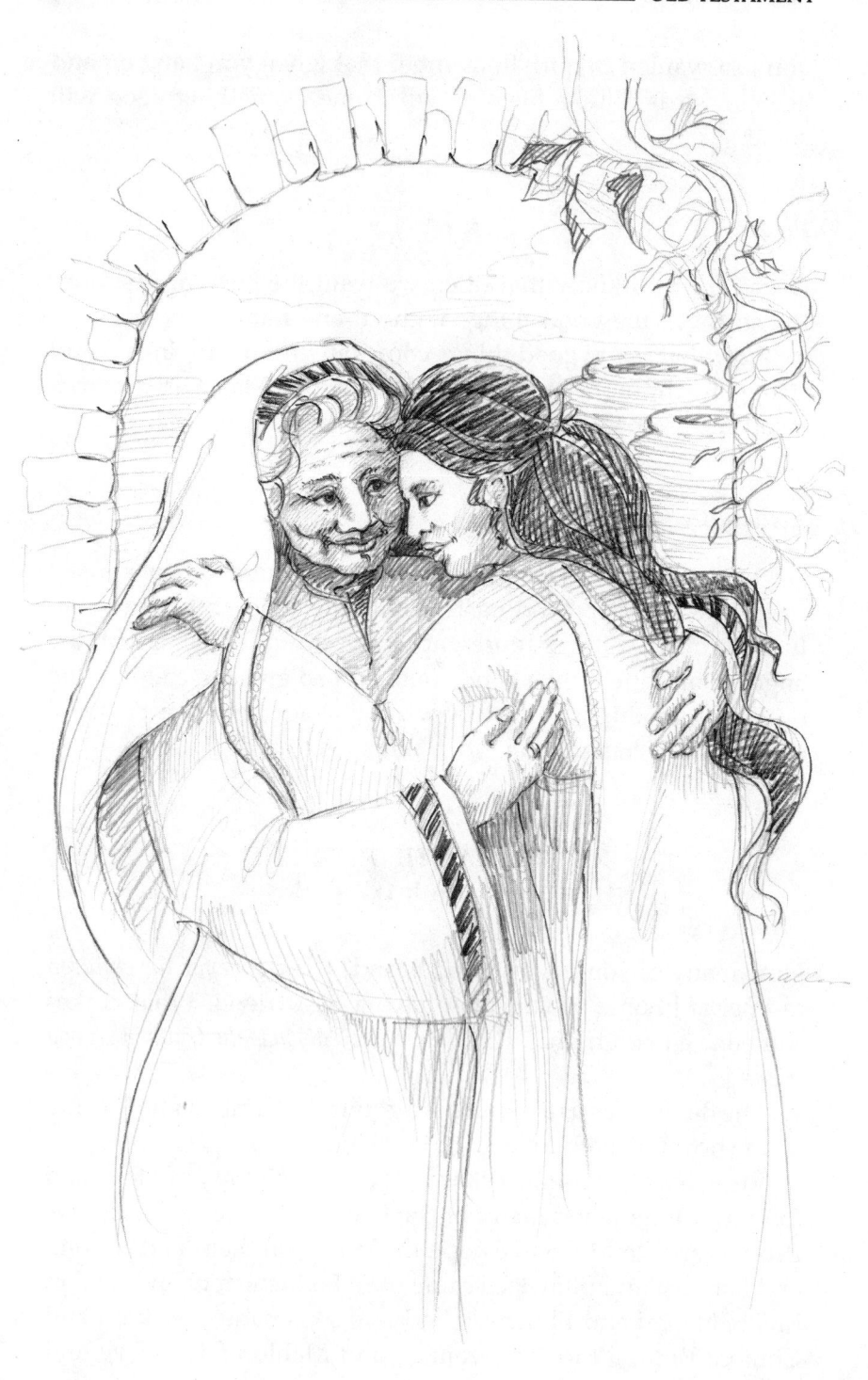

married. They didn't let their different countries and races get in the way of their love.

About ten years later Mahlon died. His brother Chilion also died. Their father Elimelech had died many years before. Now their mother Naomi was alone. She felt so sad because she had lost her husband and her two sons. Naomi decided to go back to her country of Bethlehem. She had heard that there was now food in her home country.

When Naomi got ready to leave, Ruth and Naomi's other daughter-in-law, Orpah, hugged her and cried. They loved Naomi so much and didn't want her to leave. They said to Naomi, "We want to go with you back to your country." But Naomi replied, "You're kind to me, but you'll be better off staying here in your own country." Orpah cried and kissed Naomi and then went on home.

But Ruth stayed with Naomi. She loved Naomi so much that she could not bear to leave her. Ruth wanted to be with Naomi. Ruth said to Naomi, "Don't ask me to leave you and go back home. I want to go where you go and stay where you stay." Because of her deep love for her friend, Ruth left her own country and her own people. People in Naomi's country had not always been kind to people from Ruth's country of Moab. But Ruth was willing to risk their unkindness and prejudice in order to stay with her friend. Ruth was a faithful friend.

We can see from this story of Ruth that a friend is loving and faithful. Ruth loved Naomi through good times and bad times and stayed with her. We can follow Ruth's example and stick by our friends. Even if others are mean to us, we can stand by our friends. Ruth teaches us that "a friend loves at all times" (Prov. 17:17a). Let's say this verse from the Bible together: "A friend loves at all times."

Prayer

We thank you, God, for Ruth and all she teaches us about being a faithful friend. Help us to learn to be friends who love at all times. Amen.

Activity Center

Set a up a flannel board. Place figures (made of felt or with felt strips glued to the backs) to represent Ruth and Naomi and Orpah. Also place figures of modern-day girls and boys on the board. Invite the children to take turns using the board to tell the biblical story of Ruth and Naomi. Encourage them to draw upon their imaginations to expand the biblical story of the friendship between Ruth and Naomi. Then ask them to use the figures of modern girls and boys to show how to be good friends.

COMING ALIVE (Ezekiel 37:1–14)
[*winter*]

Unless snow comes, things outside this time of year look bleak and dead. The grass is brown and dead. Most of the trees have shed their leaves. The flowers are dead. We may not be able to count on snow to brighten things up. But one thing we can count on: the grass and flowers and trees will come back to life again in the spring.

[*Pass a tulip bulb around.*] What do you think this is? [*Give the children time to respond.*] It's not very pretty, is it? It doesn't look as though it has any life in it. [*Pulling a tulip out of a sack*] Would you believe that it will become this beautiful tulip? And then next year at this time it will be dormant again and look like this bulb. "Dormant" means that it is inactive for a little while, like asleep. It may not look as though it has any life, but it does. One of the amazing things about the way God created the world is that it looks dead in the winter, but then comes back to life in the spring.

The Bible tells us that the people of Israel had become dormant. Although they believed in God, they had not been true and faithful followers of God. It was as though their faith in God had died. Ezekiel compared the Israelites to a valley full of dead bones. But God promised to bring them back to life. God's Spirit would make them come alive!

Sometimes in the church we adults get rather set in our ways and lose excitement and life in our faith. We're not dead, but sometimes we act dead and look dead. God's Spirit can make us come alive again, just as God made the Israelites come alive and God brings flowers back to life. God can use lively, bright children like each one of you to bring new life to the whole church. The more you give yourself to God and to the church, the more God will use you to help the church blossom like this beautiful tulip.

Prayer

Great Creator God, we praise you for making the world so amazing and beautiful. Use us to bring new, exciting life to the church. Amen.

Activity Center

Provide large receptacles to collect paper, aluminum cans, plastic containers, and glass containers for recycling. Explain to the children the importance of recyling waste products so that the earth God created can continue to come alive with beauty. Ask the children to collect these waste items around the church and put them in the appropriate receptacles. Encourage them to bring these waste items from home to collect. If possible, plan a field trip to a local recycling plant so that the children can observe the process.

A COURAGEOUS WOMAN
(Esther 3–8)

There is a book in the Bible called "Esther." This book is named for an important woman of courage. Esther was so brave that she risked her own life to save her people, the Jews. An evil man named Haman hated the Jewish people and plotted to kill them. Haman was a powerful man, second in command to the king. Haman thought he was really a big shot and wanted everyone else to think so too. Haman hated the Jews because one of them named Mordecai would not bow down to him. Mordecai was Esther's cousin. Haman was so furious when Mordecai would not bow down to him that he tricked the king into signing an order to destroy all the Jewish people.

Mordecai found out about Haman's evil plot and sent a messenger to Esther. He knew that Esther was the only one who could help because she was the queen. Surely she could get the king to take back his order to destroy the Jews. You see King Ahasuerus didn't know that Esther was a Jew. In those days and in that country no one could go to the king without being called. Not even the queen could go to him unless he sent for her. Those who went to the king without being called were put to death, unless the king held out the golden scepter so that they could live. This was a terrible custom. Esther sent word to her cousin Mordecai that even though she was the queen, she could not get in to see King Ahasuerus. He had not called for her in thirty days. If she went to talk to him, he might have her put to death. Mordecai encouraged Esther to risk her life to save the Jewish people. He said to her, "Who knows whether you have not come to the kingdom for such a time as this?" (Esther 4:14) So Esther drew up her courage and determined to go to the king, even though he had not sent for her. She asked Mordecai to gather all the Jews to fast and pray for her. She bravely said, "I will go to the king, though it is against the law, and if I perish, I perish" (Esther 4:16).

Three days later Esther went to see the king. You can imagine how scared she felt inside, not knowing whether he would have her killed for coming without being called. But King Ahasuerus held out the golden scepter to her, meaning that she would live. The king asked what she wanted and said that she could have anything, even half of his kingdom. Esther was so relieved and shocked that she just couldn't get out her request for the Jews. So she asked that the king and Haman come to dinner with her that night.

She planned to tell the king that Haman was plotting to kill the Jews. But that night at dinner she still couldn't bring herself to tell the king. You can imagine how much courage that would take. Haman was second in power to the king. It would be like going to tell the president of the United States that the vice-president was plotting to kill all the Texans. Now even if we knew this were true, it would take some kind of courage to tell the president. So that first night when King Ahasuerus and Haman came to dinner, all Esther could ask was that they come back to dinner the next night. The next night Esther found the courage she needed. She told the king that Haman was planning to kill all the Jewish people. The king believed Esther. He wrote an order reversing Haman's order to destroy the Jews. Esther asked the king to write this order to save the Jewish people. Because she was so brave, Esther saved the Jewish people. Esther had enough courage to risk her life to save her people.

God wants each one of us to be brave enough to stand up for what is right. We probably won't have to risk our lives, like Esther did, but it will be hard at times to stand up for what we believe and to speak up for those who need our help. As God helped Esther, God will give us the courage to do what is right.

Prayer

Strong and loving God, help us to be brave and strong enough to do what is right. Give us the courage of Esther to speak up for those who need our help. Amen.

Activity Center

Place light-weight cardboard or construction paper, scissors, colored markers, paste, and dress-up clothes and jewelry on tables. Help the children make crowns and color them. Then let them take turns dressing up and playing the parts of Queen Esther, King Ahasuerus, Mordecai, and Haman. Also invite them to act out their own experiences of standing up for what they believe.

JEALOUS BROTHERS
(Genesis 37)

See if you can solve this riddle. What do a rubber band and jealousy have in common? [*Give time for the children to answer, affirming their responses.*] One possible answer is that both a rubber band and jealousy can hurt you more than the other person. For example, a boy named Stacey was fighting with his sister Darla. Stacey got so mad at Darla that he wanted to hurt her. He tried to pop her with a rubber band. But the rubber band backfired and hit him in the eye. Stacey couldn't see out of that eye, so he went to an eye doctor. Even after two operations, Stacey still could not see out of that eye. The rubber band had made him blind in one eye.

Jealousy is like this rubber band. It can backfire on the person who is jealous. Jealousy can hurt badly. Like the rubber band destroyed Stacey's eye, jealousy can destroy relationships.

In the Bible we read about Joseph and his eleven brothers. Their father, Jacob, gave Joseph a beautiful coat. His brothers were jealous because they did not get a coat like Joseph's. Later Joseph dreamed that he was a ruler and that his brothers were bowing down to him. Instead of keeping his dreams to himself, Joseph bragged about his dreams to his brothers. These dreams made his brothers even more jealous of him. They became so jealous that they plotted to kill Joseph. They planned to kill him, throw him into some deep pit, and say that a wild beast had killed him. But one of his brothers, named Reuben, felt guilty. He talked his other brothers into throwing Joseph into the pit without killing him. Reuben planned to come back later and rescue Joseph. After Reuben had gone, the other brothers saw a group of slaves and their masters coming down the road. They thought up a way to get rid of Joseph and make money at the same time. They sold Joseph as a slave. When Reuben came back to the pit and saw that Joseph was not there, he was so upset that he tore off his clothes.

The brothers decided to take Joseph's coat and dip it in the blood of a goat. Then they took the robe back to their father. Jacob recognized the coat as Joseph's and believed that a wild beast had killed him. Jacob became so upset that he tore off his clothes and cried for his son. His sons and daughters tried to comfort him, but nobody could comfort him. He mourned and cried over Joseph for a long time. The jealousy of Joseph's brothers had backfired on them. Instead of getting more of their father's attention by getting rid of Joseph, they got less attention. Now Jacob thought about Joseph more than ever. And Reuben and his brothers felt bad for hurting Joseph and their father.

We all feel jealous sometimes. What can we do when we feel

jealous so that our jealous feelings don't backfire on us? We can think about all the good things God has given us, rather than thinking about another person who may seem to have more. We can remember that God loves each person the same. So when we feel that we have not been treated fairly, we can tell God. God understands all our feelings. God gave us our feelings. God loves us all the time and will help us love the person we're jealous of.

Prayer

God, our Helper and Friend, help us not to hurt ourselves and others when we feel jealous. Remind us of all the good things you have given each one of us. Thank you, God. Amen.

Activity Center

On tables place pencils, paper, crayons, construction paper, used magazines, scissors, and paste. Invite the children to write a story or make a picture of an experience when they felt jealous. Then seat the children in a circle and invite them to share these experiences. Encourage them to talk about how they felt, how they acted, and other ways they might have acted.

A BRAVE GIRL
(2 Kings 5:1–14)

Who can tell me what "courage" means? [*Give the children time to respond.*] We read in the Bible about many people who had courage. God helped them to be brave and to do what is right. One of these brave people was a little girl, probably around ten years old. She was a servant to some very important people. She worked for Naaman and his wife. Naaman was the commander of the army of the king of Syria. The king gave Naaman much power. But Naaman had one terrible problem. He had a disease called leprosy. Leprosy eats away at the skin and fingers and eyes. Leprosy can slowly kill a person.

The servant girl who worked for Naaman knew a prophet

named Elisha. She had heard this prophet preach about God and about how much God cares for us. She had seen God work miracles through Elisha. The little girl might have been scared to say anything to Naaman and his wife. After all, they were important people, and she was just a maid. What would they think of her, or what would they do to her if she told Naaman to go ask Elisha to cure him? What if Naaman went to Elisha and then didn't get well? Naaman might get angry at her and might even kill her. But she was a brave girl. And she cared enough about Naaman to want him to get well. So she got up her courage and said to Naaman's wife, "My lord Naaman should go to see the prophet Elisha. Elisha will cure him of his leprosy."

Naaman believed the servant girl. Naaman got fine horses and chariots and expensive gifts together and set out to find Elisha. When they got to Elisha's house, Elisha sent a messenger out to tell Naaman to go and dip himself in the Jordan River seven times. Then his leprosy would be healed. Naaman got very angry and said, "Well, the very idea. I've come all this way with fine gifts for Elisha, and Elisha won't even come out to see me himself. I thought that he would come out and just wave his hand over me,

OLD TESTAMENT ——————————————————————— 47

and I would be cured. But no! He sends a messenger out to tell me to wash in the Jordan River. Why that's the dirtiest, filthiest river there is! He tells me, an important man, to wash in some filthy river! If washing in a river could cure me, I could have found much better, cleaner rivers close to home." So Naaman stalked away, raging mad. The servant girl really was courageous to speak to him now. Naaman was so angry there was no telling what he might do. But she bravely said, "If the prophet had commanded you to do some great thing, wouldn't you have done it? Won't you just try what he says?"

So Naaman decided to try what Elisha told him to do. He went down to the Jordan River and waded out about waist deep. Then he started ducking under. One, two, three times. He looked at his skin, and he still had leprosy. Four, five, six, seven. He came up and looked at his skin. He couldn't believe what he saw! His skin was smooth and soft, just like a little child's. He was well! Naaman was cured because of the courage of the little servant girl and of the prophet Elisha. Both followed God's direction, even though Naaman got angry and might have hurt them.

We all have chances to be brave. We too can have courage. You don't have to wait until you're grown to have courage. Just as the servant girl had courage to help someone, you can be brave enough to help someone who is being treated unfairly or who is hurting in some way. You might see someone being mistreated out on the school ground. You can be brave enough to help that person or to call for help. God will help all of us to have courage.

Prayer

Dear God, help us to be brave like the servant girl. Give us courage to do what we know is right and to help people who are hurting. Amen.

Activity Center

Set up a flannel board. On the board place figures (made of felt or flannel or with felt strips glued to the backs) to represent the servant girl, Naaman, Naaman's wife, Elisha, servants, horses, and modern-day girls and boys. Also place on the flannel board representations of the Jordan River with trees around it. Invite the children to take turns telling the story of the brave servant girl and Naaman. Then ask them to use the figures of modern-day girls and boys to tell about a time when they showed courage.

SLIME OR ROCK
(1 Kings 18:20–40)

In this hand I have a rock. And in this other hand I hold something called "slime." [*"Slime" or "ectoplasm" can be purchased from a toy store.*] Have any of you ever played with slime? Since the movie *Ghostbusters* came out, toy stores have been selling this slime. Reach in this container and feel it. [*Let the children feel the slime.*] How does it feel to you? [*Give the children a chance to respond.*] This slime oozes all over whatever you put it on. It takes the shape of whatever you put it in. [*Put the slime in containers of various shapes.*] If you put it in a round container, it becomes round. If you put it in a square container, it becomes square. See how it does.

Now this rock never changes shape. [*Put the rock in the containers of various shapes.*] No matter where you put it, it never changes. It's firm and hard, not drippy and slimy. [*Let the children feel the rock.*] This rock knows what it is. It's not like the slime that keeps changing shapes.

There was an Israelite prophet named Elijah, who was like this rock. He stayed firm in his belief in God, no matter where he was. There were other Israelite people who said that they believed in God, but they went along with whoever was around them. These people were in a country where most of the people worshipped the false god Baal. Most of the Israelites went back and forth between worshipping the true God and the false god Baal. They were like this dripping, oozing slime. They were molded by what was around them. They just "slimed" back and forth between one belief and the other. But the prophet Elijah kept believing in the true God, no matter who was around. Elijah was like this rock.

God wants us to be like a rock, not like slime. Sometimes we have trouble doing what we know God wants us to do when our friends around us are doing something else. It's easy just to go along with the crowd, to be like slime and take the shape of whatever and whoever are close by. But God will help us to be strong like a rock, to stand up for our beliefs, no matter what people around us say or do.

Prayer

We thank you that you are like a Rock, that you never change in your love for us. God, please help us to be strong like a rock in our love for you. Amen.

Activity Center

Place different kinds of leaves, flowers, grass, thorns, rocks, vegetables, seeds, water, and other natural things on tables. Also provide magic markers, crayons, water colors, construction paper, paste, and scissors. Talk about God's creation of everything and the messages God gives us through some of these things. Invite the children to feel the natural objects and talk about them. Ask the children if they remind us of anything God wants us to be like, or not be like. Encourage the children to make their own creations using the natural things, along with the markers, paper, etc.

GROWING THROUGH SHARING
(1 Kings 17:8–16)

The Bible tells us about a woman who lived in a city called Zarephath in the country of Israel. The Bible doesn't tell us her name. But we do learn that she was a widow; that is, her husband had died. She had a son and other members of the household who lived with her. In the country where she lived it had not rained for a long time. Without rain the crops could not grow, so there was not enough food.

One day the prophet Elijah came to Zarephath. As he was

entering the city, he saw this woman gathering sticks. He was hungry and thirsty from his journey, so he asked her for some bread and water. She replied, "I don't have anything baked. All I have left is a handful of meal in a jar, and a little oil. And I have a son to feed. So I am gathering a few sticks so that I can build a fire and cook one last piece of bread for my son and me. Then I guess we'll starve to death." Elijah said to her, "Don't be afraid. First, make a little bread for me and then make some for your son and for yourself. Just trust God that there will be enough." So she trusted God and made a piece of bread for Elijah.

[*Dramatize this story.*] To see what happened, let's pretend that I am the woman, and you be Elijah, and you be the woman's son. [*Pick a child to be Elijah and another to be the woman's son.*] The rest of you be other members of her household. Here is the jar with the handful of meal. [*Hold up the jar with about a half cup of corn meal.*] First, I take enough meal to make some bread for Elijah. Then I make some for my son. [*Pour meal into bowl and pretend to make bread. Keep the children's attention focused on this action, while a child, instructed ahead of time, fills the jar with meal.*] Then I look in the jar expecting it to be empty, because I had only enough for two. But to my amazement, the jar is full! I have more than I started with. So I feed the other members of the household and myself, and there's still enough to feed everyone for many days.

God kept filling that woman's jar over and over again so that she had enough food until rain came and made the crops grow again. Because she was willing to share what little she had, God blessed what she had and made it grow and grow. If she had kept the meal for herself, she and her son would have starved to death.

Whatever God has given us is to share with others, not just to keep for ourselves. God has given each one of us many gifts. God wants us to use these gifts to help others. Then these gifts will grow and grow, just like the meal in the woman's jar.

Let's say this verse together: "God loves a cheerful giver" (2 Cor. 9:7).

Prayer

God, we thank you for the example of this woman who shared her food with Elijah. Help us to share what you have given us with people in need. Amen.

Activity Center

Place dress-up clothes on table. Invite the children to take turns dressing like they think Elijah, the widow, and the son would have dressed. Then have them act out the story while another child reads the account from 1 Kings 17:8–16.

NEW TESTAMENT STORIES AND SERMONS

THE PRODIGAL DAUGHTER
(Luke 15:11–32)

There once was a nine-year-old girl named Glenda. She had a brother named Tom, who was eleven. Tom did well in school. He always did what his teachers told him to do, so he never got in trouble at school. And at home he did what his parents told him to do. He had chores around the house, like taking out the garbage, cleaning his room, and washing the dishes. He always did these jobs without being told. Tom's little sister, Glenda, was plenty smart too. But she didn't make good grades because she turned assignments in late and didn't study for tests. Also she got in trouble for talking out-of-turn and passing notes in class. Glenda gave her parents trouble too. She argued with them. Her parents had to tell her over and over to do her chores, and still she would not always do them. Most of the time her room looked like a junk yard. To help Glenda learn to do better, her parents took away some of her privileges, like watching TV and going to friends' houses.

Instead of helping Glenda, Tom bragged about how much better he was. When they brought home report cards, he'd say, "I got all 'As.' What did you get, Glenda?" And he would come in her room and say, "Your room looks terrible. Why can't you be like me and keep your room clean? I do what Mom and Dad say, and you don't. You need to be more like me."

One Saturday morning when she had gotten just about enough of Tom, Glenda decided to run away from home. She left a note that said, "Dear Mother and Daddy, Tom is good, and I'm bad. One good kid is enough for you. You don't need me around anymore. Love, Glenda." Glenda's parents were terribly upset when they found the note. They started frantically looking for Glenda. All day long they looked and looked. They called all her friends and even called the police to search for her — but no Glenda. They were worried to death. Finally at about eight o'clock that night, they saw Glenda walking toward the house. They ran and hugged and kissed her and told her how glad they were that she was back. She said, "I'm so sorry I scared you. I'm going to try to do better from now on." They forgave her and said, "Let's plan a party to celebrate!"

But Tom got mad and said, "Well, I've been good all this time, and you never gave me a party. Glenda's been the bad one, and you're giving her a party!" Tom's mother and father said to him, "We've given you good things all your life. Can't you be happy with us that Glenda is home safely and wants to act better now?" But Tom stayed mad and wouldn't even go to the party.

Which one did wrong — Glenda or Tom? [*Help the children to see that both did wrong.*] Glenda disobeyed her parents and teachers. She wasted the good mind God gave her by not studying and doing her best in school. Tom had bad attitudes. He bragged to Glenda about how much better he was and got jealous when their parents gave Glenda a party. Glenda told her parents that she was sorry, and they forgave her. Tom needed to say that he was sorry too. His parents would have forgiven him. Like these parents, God will always forgive us for disobeying and for having bad attitudes.

In the Bible we find a story much like this one. It is called the parable of the prodigal son. "Prodigal" means wasteful. The son in the Bible story wasted his father's money, like Glenda wasted her mind and abilities. The father in the Bible story forgave the prodigal son, just like Glenda's parents forgave their prodigal daughter.

We are all daughters and sons of our Mother and Father God. At times we all waste the gifts God gives us. And we do other wrong things and fail to do the good things God wants us to do. But our Father and Mother God will forgive us and help us to do better.

Prayer

Our Mother and Father in heaven, thank you for loving us and forgiving us, no matter what we do. Forgive us when we have not done what you want us to do. Help us to use the gifts you have given us. Amen.

Activity Center

Invite the children to act out the story of the "prodigal daughter" or the "prodigal son." Give the children the opportunity to experience each of the characters: the prodigal daughter or son, the haughty son or daughter, and the forgiving mother or father. Then seat the children in a circle and ask them to talk about their feelings in each of these roles.

A WOMAN WHO BUILT A CHURCH
(Acts 16:11–15, 40)

What is a church? [*Give the children time to respond.*] When we talk about "going to church," we're usually talking about the church building. But a church is not a building. A church is a group of people, a group of people who follow Christ. So building a church means bringing together a group of people who follow Christ.

Lydia built a church. She started the first church in Europe, in the city of Philippi. Lydia was a successful businesswoman, a seller of purple dye and purple cloth. Kings and queens and other important people wore purple. Lydia traded with these important people. But no matter how rich and important she was, her heart longed for something more. Her heart longed to know God.

Lydia brought together a group of people to pray and seek

God. They didn't meet inside a building. They met by the river at Philippi. One Sabbath day this group was meeting. Missionaries Paul and Silas came by and joined this prayer group. Paul told the group the Good News that they could find a close relationship with God through Jesus Christ. God opened Lydia's heart, and she believed Paul's message about Christ's love. Soon afterward, she was baptized as a Christian. Lydia led the other members of her household to believe in Christ and to be baptized. Lydia invited Paul and Silas to stay in her home. Here in Lydia's home the first church in Philippi, and in all Europe, began.

Lydia built this first church beginning with the members of her own household. This first church in Europe did not begin in a huge, expensive building, but in the home of Lydia. This church began with a small group of people who believed in Christ and decided to follow Christ.

Churches today begin in the same way. You can build a church. I can build a church. We can build a church by bringing together a group of people who follow Christ.

NEW TESTAMENT _____ 57

Prayer

We thank you, God, for Lydia, who built the first church in Europe. Help us to be church builders right where we are, in Christ's name. Amen.

Activity Center

Seat the children in a circle. Invite them to take turns being the leader. Instruct the leader to stand in the middle of the circle and build a church with the children. Help them to act out ways that they can be the church together.

EACH ONE IMPORTANT
(1 Corinthians 12:12–27)

Let's sing along with some songs I have on this tape. [*Put the tape in a tape player that has one battery burned out.*] First, I'll play the tape, and then we'll sing along.

Oh no, something's wrong! It's not playing. What do you think is wrong with this tape player? What should I do? [*Let the children suggest several things to do.*] Let's make sure the tape is in right. [*Take the tape out and put it back in.*] Now I know it's in right. I need to make sure that I press "play," not "rewind," or another one of these buttons. It's still not playing. What's wrong? Maybe I should check the batteries. I brought along a spare battery just in case. I'll try taking this battery out and putting in a new one. [*Replace the burned-out battery, but put it in the wrong way.*] Now let's try to play it. Surely it will work this time. Oh no! It's still not working! [*Check the battery again.*] Oh, I see what's wrong. I put the new battery in the wrong way. Let's turn it around and see if that makes any difference. [*Turn the player on, and play the tape.*] Finally, it works!

A church is like this tape player in many ways. The members of the church are like the parts of the tape player. When one of the batteries was not working, it wouldn't play. The three other batteries were working just fine, and all the other parts inside the player were working fine. It's hard to believe that just one little battery not doing its job could mess up the whole works. But that's what happened. And the battery had to be put in just right before it would work. It's the same way in the church. It takes each member to make it work right. And all the members need to be doing just what God wants them to be doing. All need to be using their special gifts and working in the place God wants them.

The Bible compares the members of the church to the parts of a body. Each part of the body is important. God created our bodies so that each part has an important job to do. If one part of the body does not work right, then the whole body suffers. You probably have stubbed your toe, and your whole body hurt. The church is the same way. Each one of us in the church is important. God has given each one of us special gifts and special jobs to do. If one of us does not do her or his job right, then the whole church suffers. But when all of us do the jobs God has for us, then the church grows strong and healthy. Each one of us is so important to the church.

Prayer

How thankful we are, God, that you give each one of us important work to do in the church. Help us to do our part well so that the church will be strong and healthy. Amen.

Activity Center

On tables place drawing paper, construction paper, magic markers, crayons, used Sunday School curriculum literature, used magazines, scissors, and paste. Ask the children to draw pictures or make collages illustrating the various jobs in a church. Invite each child to tell the group what job he or she is doing now, or would like to do in the future.

SWEET TARTS AND FAITH
(Mark 9:14–24)

What are some foods that taste sweet? What foods taste sour? [*Give time for the children to respond.*] Can something taste sweet and sour at the same time? [*Give each child a sweet tart.*] Now close your eyes and concentrate on the taste of the sweet tart. How many of you think it tastes sweet? How many of you think it tastes sour? It's hard to decide because it tastes sweet and sour at the same time. That's why it's called a "sweet tart." "Tart" means sour.

We usually think of sweet and sour as opposites, as completely different, like night and day. Do you think that you can like people and not like them at the same time? Those are two different feelings, aren't they? But it is possible to like and dislike at the same time. We all have these feelings even toward the people we love most. Like our mothers or fathers or brothers or sisters. There are some things we might not like about them. And there are times we get mad at them and don't like them much at all. But that doesn't mean that we don't also love them. Just like the sweet tart can be sweet and sour at the same time, you can like and not like someone at the same time.

When you come to church, you hear people talk about faith in God. What do you think "faith" means? [*Give time for the children to respond.*] When you have faith in God, does that mean that you believe in God all the time? Is it possible to believe and not believe at the same time? In the Bible there is a story about a man who brings his son to Jesus to be healed. The son has been sick a long time. Jesus asks the father to believe that he can heal the son. The father says that he believes in Jesus, but at the same time is having trouble believing. He says, "I believe; help my unbelief!" (Mark 9:24). He is honest in telling Jesus that he is believing and not believing at the same time. Even though the father has trouble believing, Jesus still heals the boy. Jesus understands when we have trouble believing. Jesus wants us to ask questions when we're having trouble believing. We encourage you to ask questions about things you don't understand about God. Your faith in God will grow as you ask questions about what you have a hard time believing.

Now you can solve this riddle. How are sweet tarts and faith alike? [*Give time for the children to respond.*] Both bring opposites together. Sweet tarts can taste sweet and sour at the same time, and at the same time we can not believe and believe in God.

Prayer

Understanding God, we thank you that we can tell you everything we're thinking and feeling. We believe in you, but we have trouble believing at times. Help us to ask questions so that we can understand you better. Amen.

Activity Center

Place objects that represent opposites on tables: for example, pictures of night and day and of other opposites, hot and cold water, wet and dry cloth, sugar and vinegar, big and little objects. Provide paper, scissors, paste, bowls, etc. Have the children experiment with bringing these opposites together. Encourage the children to create and talk about their creations. Why do you suppose God made opposites? What would the world be like without opposites? Help the children see the beauty and richness of diversity.

THREE KINDS OF SOIL
(Matthew 13:3–9)

Jesus used parables to teach people. A parable is a story that helps us understand about God and about doing what God wants us to do. A parable is an earthly story with a heavenly meaning. Jesus used things we can see and touch, like seeds and coins, to help us understand about God whom we can't see.

I want you to help me act out one of Jesus' parables. I need a sower, someone who plants seeds. [*Ask one of the children to be the sower and give her or him some seeds.*] Now I need three of you to hold the different kinds of soil. [*Give three children a small container each, one with rocky soil, another with thorny soil, and another with good soil.*]

Jesus told this story about the sower and the seeds. The sower went out to plant seeds. Some seed fell along the path. [*Tell the sower to drop some seeds on the floor.*] Other seeds fell on rocky soil. [*The sower drops some seeds in the rocky soil container.*] These seeds started growing. But when the sun got hot, these plants died because they had no root. Other seeds fell on soil that had thorns and weeds. [*The sower drops some seeds in the container with thorny soil.*] These seeds started growing, but the thorns and weeds choked the plants, and they died. Other seeds fell on good soil. [*The sower drops some seeds in the container with dark, rich soil.*] These seeds grew into healthy, strong plants. They produced grain for bread and produced more seeds that grew into more healthy plants.

Jesus told the disciples what this parable means. The seed is like God's word. The soil is like different kinds of people and the ways they receive God's word. Some seed fell along the path; it didn't have any soil at all to grow in. This would be like people who don't receive God's word at all. Maybe they hear some preacher on TV or radio say something about God's word. But they never read the Bible or think about God themselves. So they really don't have any soil for God's word to grow in. Some seeds, you remember, fell on rocky soil. [*Pass around the rocky soil for the children to see and touch.*] The rocky soil has a thin layer of good soil on top, so the seeds grow up quickly. But the seeds die because the plants can't get their roots down deeply enough into the rocky soil. This soil is like people who get all excited about God's word when they first hear it. They are eager to do God's work. But when the work gets hard and not too much fun, or when their friends make fun of them for doing something good, they just quit. Then there were the seeds that fell on soil with thorns and weeds. [*Pass around the thorny soil for the children to see and touch.*] The seeds started to grow, but the weeds choked them. This soil is like people who hear God's word and start doing what God wants them to. But then they let other things get in the way. They become more interested in being popular or making money or just having a good time. But remember that some seeds fell on good soil. See how dark and rich this soil looks. [*Pass around the good soil for the children to see and touch.*] This good soil is like people who hear God's word and do what God says, even when it is hard and unpopular. These people grow to be strong in caring for people and making the world a better place. They help other people become the best they can be.

God wants each one of us to be like the good soil. The Bible tells us to be doers of the word and not hearers only. This means that we need to learn what God's word says and do what it says, not just listen to it and forget it. Let's say this verse together: "Be doers of the word and not hearers only" (James 1:22). Let's pray this verse together: "God, help us to be doers of the word and not hearers only."

Activity Center

Inside a gold-colored box, place green felt to represent grass. Make trees out of brown felt for the trunks and lighter green felt for the leaves. Make flowers from felt of various bright colors. Place different kinds of soil in the box. Place a container of seeds outside the box. Let the children take turns telling the parable of the sower, using the box and the seeds. Then encourage them to create new stories using the box and seeds.

WHO GAVE THE MOST?
(Luke 21:1–4)

Do you like puzzles? See if you can figure out this puzzle. Listen carefully. Three children named Theo, Vanessa, and Jesse did jobs around the house to earn money. Theo earned $10.00 every week. Vanessa earned $2.00, and Jesse earned $.50. The reason Theo earned more was not that he worked that much harder, but that his parents had more money to pay him. Theo and Vanessa and Jesse had learned in Sunday School how important it is to give money to God's work in the church. So each one brought money to church. Theo had $10.00, and he decided to bring $1.00 to church. [*Demonstrate this by placing ten dollar bills on your lap or on a table and taking one out.*] Vanessa had $2.00 or eight quarters, and she decided to give $.50, or two quarters. [*Demonstrate with eight quarters.*] Jesse had $.50, or two quarters, and he gave one quarter. [*Demonstrate with two quarters.*] Now who gave the most? [*Give time for the children to respond.*] Jesse gave the most. Even though he gave only one quarter, he gave the most. Why did he give the most? [*Let the children respond.*] There's no trick in this puzzle. Jesse gave the most in God's eyes because he gave half of what he had. Most people would think that Theo gave the most because everyone knows that a dollar is more than a quarter. And they would think that Vanessa gave more than Jesse, because two quarters are more than one quarter. But God measures what we give not by how large the gift is, but by how much we have to give. If God has given us a lot of money to take care of, then God expects us to give a lot. God does not expect the person who does not have much money to give as much.

The Bible tells about a time when Jesus was watching people bring their offerings to church. Jesus saw all the rich people putting in large amounts of money. Then Jesus saw a poor widow bring two small coins, about like pennies. Jesus said that the widow gave more than all the rich people. They gave only a little of all that they had. They still had a great deal of money left. But the widow gave all that she had. She gave the most.

God wants each of us to give to God's work in the church. You don't have to wait until you grow up to give. You can begin to give now. You may not have much money. If you get an allowance, you can give part of that money. Or you can earn money by doing jobs for your parents or your neighbors. Remember that the important thing is not how much you give, but what you give out of what you have.

Prayer

We thank you, God, for all your gifts to us. Help us to learn to give to you, in Christ's name. Amen.

Activity Center

Place paper money on tables. Help the children to act out the story of Theo, Vanessa, and Jesse, so that they understand why Jesse gave the most. Ask them to figure 10 percent, 25 percent, and 50 percent of various amounts of money. Talk about how to decide how much they should give.

FULL SACKS AND BARNS (Luke 12:16–21)
[appropriate near Halloween or Valentine's Day]

One year on Halloween two children named John and Martha got lots and lots of candy. John went to Halloween parties at school and at church and got candy. [*Start putting candy in a sack.*] Then his grandparents gave him Halloween candy. [*Put more candy in the sack.*] Then he went "Trick or Treating" and got more candy. [*Put candy in the sack until it overflows.*] Soon he had so much candy, his bag overflowed. He asked himself, "Where can I put all this candy?" Then he decided to throw his sack away and get a larger sack. [*Put the candy in a larger sack.*] Then he thought, "Now I have enough candy to last a long time, maybe all year."

John's friend Martha also went to Halloween parties and got lots of candy. [*Start putting candy in a sack.*] Then she went "Trick or Treating," and got more candy. [*Keep putting candy in the sack.*] Then her grandparents and other relatives gave her candy. [*Put candy in the sack until it overflows.*] Soon her sack was full and overflowing, just like John's. Martha had so much candy. She asked herself, "Where can I put all this candy?" All of a sudden she remembered that her Sunday School class had made Christmas cards for children in the hospital last year. So she thought, "I bet there are many children in the hospital who didn't get to go to Halloween parties and "Trick or Treating." I don't need all this candy. I think I'll ask my parents to take me to the hospital so that I can give some of my candy to the children."

Jesus told a parable about a farmer who was much like John. This farmer's land produced more food than he could hold in his barns. His barns were full and overflowing. So he decided to tear down those barns and build larger barns. Then he would have enough food for many years, without even working. He wanted to keep everything for himself. Jesus said that this farmer was foolish.

God wants us to share with other people. The farmer should have shared with hungry people instead of keeping all the food for himself. God does not want us to be like the stingy farmer and like John who kept everything they had for themselves. God wants us to be like Martha, who shared her candy with children who didn't have any. God has given us so much. God wants us to share with others.

Prayer

Thank you, God, for giving us so many good things. Help us to share what we have with others. Amen.

Activity Center

Place candy and sacks on tables. Invite the children to act out the stories of John and Martha. Ask them to talk about other ways they might have shared their candy. Give the children some candy, and ask them to share it with children who don't have any.

SAYING "THANK YOU" TO GOD (Luke 17:11–19)
[*appropriate near Thanksgiving Day*]

One day Jesus was walking to Jerusalem and saw ten people who had leprosy. Leprosy is a terrible sickness that causes rough, scaly sores on the skin. Leprosy can eat away at a hand or foot until it's no more than a stump. Not many people have this disease today. But in Jesus' day it was more common. And people back then thought it was contagious. They called lepers "unclean" and made them stay out of the city, off by themselves. The ten lepers Jesus met would not come close to him because they thought they were "unclean." So they called out to Jesus, "Please, help us, Jesus!" Jesus cared for them and healed them. I'm sure all ten felt glad to be cured of that terrible disease. But only one man did something to show that he was thankful. He went back to Jesus and fell down at Jesus' feet. He thanked Jesus and praised Jesus for healing him. Jesus was glad that he came back to say "thank you." But Jesus asked, "Where are the other nine lepers I healed? Why didn't they also return and say 'thank you'?" Jesus felt sad that they had not said "thank you."

There are many ways we can say "thank you" to God. A girl named Rosemary became sick with asthma when she was five years old. This sickness made it hard for her to breathe. Sometimes she had such a hard time breathing that she had to go to the hospital. Her parents took her to many different doctors to see if they could make her well. But Rosemary continued to have asthma attacks. Once when she was ten years old, the asthma developed into pneumonia. Rosemary was in the hospital for many weeks. There in the hospital Rosemary asked God to help her get well, to help the doctors and nurses know what to do for her. Before long, Rosemary began to get better. Soon she got to go home from the hospital and back to school. She was so glad to see all her friends again. She thanked God for making her well. She wanted to do something to show God how thankful she was. She decided she would grow up and become a doctor so that she could help other sick people. So she studied hard in school, and then went on to college and medical school. She became a fine, caring doctor who helped many people. This was Rosemary's way of saying, "Thank you, God, for making me well and strong."

There are many ways we can say "thank you" to God. We can say "thank you" when we pray. Let's thank God right now. [*Invite the children to say prayers of thanks to God.*] We can say "thank you" by helping other people. We can say "thank you" to God by thanking people who help us.

Activity Center

Give each child a thank-you note, or help the children make thank-you notes from construction paper, drawing paper, and colored pencils. Ask the children to think of people who have helped them and then to choose one to write. Encourage the children to ask their parent(s) to help them mail the thank-you notes.

GOD COMES TO US
(Romans 1:19–20; John 1:1–18)
[*Advent*]

This is a special time of year. We are beginning Advent. What does "Advent" mean? The word "Advent" means "coming." Advent is that time before Christmas when we prepare to celebrate the coming of Christ into our world. Let's start preparing to celebrate Christ's coming by thinking of all the ways God comes to us.

Does God come to us like a great big Superman or Wonder Woman and do spectacular things? God can do things even more spectacular than what Wonder Woman and Superman do, but God does not always choose to work this way. What are other ways God comes to us? [*Give time for the children to respond.*]

God comes to us through the marvelous plants and animals and stars and other things God has created. The Bible tells us that even though we cannot see God, we can know much about God through the beautiful world God created. God comes to us through something as simple as a pecan. [*Show the children a pecan; then crack it and have them look inside.*] Look closely at this pecan. Can you believe that from this small pecan a huge pecan tree will grow? And inside this shell is a delicious nut that makes chocolate chip cookies and chocolate fudge taste so good. [*Give each child a piece of pecan or a chocolate chip cookie to eat.*] Pecans are amazing! You can't make a pecan. I can't make one. Nobody but God, the great Creator, can make a pecan. Now look at these leaves. [*Show the children several leaves from one kind of tree.*] These leaves are from the same tree. But they are not alike. No two leaves are exactly alike. The pattern of veins in each leaf is different. [*Pass the leaves around and ask the children to look closely at the pattern of the veins.*] When you think about how many trees there are in the world and how many leaves on each tree, that is truly amazing! When we look at what God has made, we can see something of God. We see that God is brilliant and creative, and that She likes variety and beauty. We see that God wants us to enjoy what She has created. God comes to us and shows us love through the creation.

Another way God comes to us is through other people. How many of you saw grandparents and other relatives over the Thanksgiving holidays? Did you feel how much they love you? God comes to us through the love of our families. God comes to us through people who help us. [*Show the children pictures of people at church helping others. If possible, show pictures with the children in them. Show pictures of adults teaching them in Sunday School or Vacation Bible School. Show church members delivering Meals on Wheels or visiting in nursing homes or involved in other ministries. Show children singing in the choir or helping in some way at church.*] God is at work in all these ways. Anytime we are helping people, showing love, making peace, praising God, developing talents, God is at work in us. God works in us when we help others and comes to us through people who help us.

At this time of year we especially celebrate God's coming to us through Jesus Christ. Almost two thousand years ago, God came into our world in the form of a tiny baby born in a stable surrounded by cows and sheep and donkeys. An unlikely place for God to come! Many people didn't believe that this baby was God. They expected God to come in the form of a great king in a huge palace. Christ still comes to us in unexpected ways and places. Many times we don't recognize Christ today, because we're looking in the wrong places. We may be looking for Christ only in big churches and in rich, well-dressed people. But Christ still comes in lowly places and in poor and hurting people. As we prepare for the celebration of Christmas, let's open our eyes to Christ around us.

Sing "Child in the Manger" as a closing prayer (page 139).

Activity Center

Provide used curriculum literature and magazines, scissors, paste, water colors, magic markers, and poster board or butcher paper. Ask the children to find pictures of people helping others in various ways and to cut them out to make posters entitled "God Comes to Us." Then encourage the children to make posters with

NEW TESTAMENT _____ 69

their own drawings or paintings showing ways God comes to us (through nature and people).

NO ROOM (Luke 2:1–7)
[Advent or Christmas]

Let's use our imaginations to take us back to Bethlehem almost two thousand years ago when Jesus was born. Mary and Joseph lived in a small town called Nazareth. Nine months earlier an angel had appeared to Mary and then to Joseph telling them that they would be parents of an extraordinary child. And now it was almost time for the baby to be born. Mary and Joseph learned that they would have to make a trip to Bethlehem. The emperor ordered all people to go to the cities their families were from so that they could be counted for taxes.

How did Mary and Joseph go from Nazareth to Bethlehem? Did they go in a big car? No, they had to ride on a donkey. It was about thirty miles from Nazareth to Bethlehem. That wouldn't take long in a car, but it was a long day's journey on a donkey. They had to travel slowly over the dusty, rocky road because Mary was about to have a baby. You can imagine how tired Mary and Joseph felt.

When they finally arrived in Bethlehem, they went to the Bethlehem inn to find a room for the night. You can imagine this inn. It may have looked something like our motels or hotels today, only without electric lights or running water. The Bible tells us that there was no room for Mary and Joseph in the inn. It doesn't tell us anything about the innkeeper, but we can use our imaginations to see what this person may have been like. Joseph and Mary probably asked the innkeeper, "Do you have a room for us to stay tonight?" What do you think the innkeeper said? What would you have said if you had been the innkeeper? The innkeeper probably said something like this: "I can't give you anything. Can't you see the inn is full? People have been coming all day long from many different places to be counted for the taxes. There is just no room for you." Mary and Joseph probably got upset and said, "But we have to find some place to stay! The night will be cold. And we're about to have a baby. Can't you see?" Finally the innkeeper replied, "The only place I can give you is out in the barn." So Mary and Joseph had to go out to sleep in the stable with the cows and sheep and horses.

There in that stable Jesus was born. Mary and Joseph had no crib or baby bed for Jesus. The only thing they could find was a manger, something like this. [*Show the children a picture of a manger, or a life-size or miniature wooden manger from a nativity scene.*] Does anyone know what a manger was used for? It held food for cows and horses. Here was Jesus, lying in an animal feeding trough. Many people came to worship Jesus. A big star shone over the stable to point the way to Jesus. The innkeeper probably went out to see what was going on. Maybe then the innkeeper began to realize that this was a great person who had been born out in the barn. Perhaps the innkeeper thought: "If only I had known, I would have made room for Mary and Joseph, even if I had to give them my own room."

Christ Jesus comes to us today, wanting to find room in our hearts. We can be like the innkeeper, and say, "There's no room for you here." Or we can say, "Come on in. I'll give you the most important place in my heart."

Prayer

Come into our hearts, Christ Jesus. There is room in our hearts for you. Amen.

Sing "There Is Room in My Heart" or "Into My Heart" (pages 150 and 152).

Activity Center

Place dress-up clothes on tables. Invite the children to take turns dressing up like they think Mary, Joseph, and the innkeeper might have dressed. Have them act out the story of Mary and Joseph coming to the inn in Bethlehem and finding no room. Encourage them to use their imaginations to develop the conversation between the innkeeper and Mary and Joseph.

A NEW KIND OF LEADER (Matthew 21:1–11)
[Palm Sunday]

Do you know why we call today "Palm Sunday"? [*Give the children time to respond.*] Today we are celebrating the day Jesus rode into Jerusalem to the cheering of children and adults and the spreading of palm branches on the road. We call this the "Triumphal Entry" of Jesus. But Jesus didn't ride into Jerusalem in a big brand new Cadillac or a limousine, as important people would today. Jesus didn't even ride on a splendid, prancing horse, as important people did back then. Jesus rode into Jerusalem on a donkey, which his disciples had borrowed for him.

Jesus had been resting in the village of Bethany with his friends Mary, Martha, and Lazarus. Jesus asked two disciples to go into another village and borrow a donkey. Jesus could have chosen the finest horse to ride into Jerusalem. But he chose a little donkey. One reason is that the donkey is a symbol of peace. And Jesus came to bring peace and to make us peacemakers. Also Jesus wanted people to know that he wasn't the kind of leader they were used to, the kind who wanted power and fame. Jesus was more interested in serving people, in helping people, and in giving to people than in being big and important. Jesus was a new kind of leader, the kind who serves people instead of bosses people.

When Jesus rode into the big city of Jerusalem on the little donkey, crowds of people followed. They knew that Jesus was special in a new way. They had seen Jesus perform miracles, such as healing people. And they had seen Jesus helping poor people, people others looked down on. They knew there was something different about Jesus. So they were excited to see Jesus. They threw their coats down in the road to show that they were honoring Jesus. They cut off branches from palm trees and spread them along the road for Jesus. Palm branches are a sign of victory. The children and grown-ups shouted, "Hosanna in the Highest!" "Hosanna" means "praise God." This was a time of victory for Jesus. The people praised Jesus.

On this Sunday before Easter we celebrate the time when Jesus rode into Jerusalem, and the people praised Jesus and spread palm branches. That's why we call this Sunday "Palm Sunday."

Jesus wants each one of us to be a new kind of leader, the kind of leader who helps needy people. Jesus leads people to peace instead of to war. Jesus wins victories over wrong. When we follow Jesus, we will be this new kind of leader.

Prayer

We thank you for teaching us a new kind of leadership. Help us to follow you, Jesus Christ. Amen.

Activity Center

On tables place paper, pens, colored pencils, and colored markers. Invite the children to list or draw pictures of ways they can follow Jesus in being a new kind of leader. Encourage the children to choose one of these actions to do in the next week.

MARY MAGDALENE AND BUTTERFLIES (John 20:1–18)
[*Easter*]

What do butterflies and Mary Magdalene have in common? [*Show the children a picture of Mary Magdalene and a real butterfly or a picture of a butterfly.*] They don't exactly look alike, do they? But they do have something in common. Mary Magdalene was the first witness of the resurrection. She was the first person to see Christ after Christ came back to life. Butterflies have become a symbol of the resurrection.

Mary Magdalene was one of Jesus' closest followers. She was a disciple of Jesus. She followed Jesus, giving Jesus money and helping to spread the Good News of Jesus' love for everyone (Luke 8:1–3). Mary Magdalene loved Jesus. She loved Jesus so much that she stood by Jesus when he was being crucified, even though many of the other disciples ran away because they were afraid for their lives (Matt. 27:55–56).

After Jesus died, Mary Magdalene felt very sad and alone. She had put so much hope in Jesus. She was sure that Jesus was going to change the world. And now it was all over. Jesus was dead.

NEW TESTAMENT — 73

She still couldn't believe it. She cried all day and into the night, but nothing could make her feel better. Jesus was gone forever.

Two days later, on a Sunday morning, Mary Magdalene and some other women went to Jesus' grave to put sweet-smelling spices on the body. She thought it might help to say "goodbye" to Jesus once more. But when she got to the tomb, she saw that the stone had been taken away. Back then, people were buried in cave-like tombs that were closed with big stones. [*Show a picture.*] Mary Magdalene looked inside the tomb and did not see Jesus' body. So she ran and told two other disciples. They came back with Mary to the tomb and looked in with her. They saw the cloths that had been wrapped around Jesus' body. But Jesus' body was not there.

Mary Magdalene didn't know what to think. She stood outside

the tomb crying. It was bad enough that Jesus had died. And now someone had stolen Jesus' body. As she cried, she looked into the tomb once more to see if she could find the body. This time she saw two angels, sitting where the body of Jesus had lain. They said to her, "Woman, why are you crying?" She replied, "Because they have taken Jesus' body away, and I don't know where they have put it." Then she turned around and saw Jesus standing behind her, but she didn't know it was Jesus. After all, she thought Jesus was dead. Jesus said to her, "Woman, why are you crying? Who are you looking for?" She still didn't recognize Jesus. She thought that Jesus was the gardener. She said, "If you have carried away Jesus' body, tell me where you have laid it." Jesus said to her, "Mary." At that moment when Jesus called her name, she knew! Jesus had come back to life and was standing right there calling her name. She just couldn't believe it! But she knew for sure that it was Jesus. Mary was so excited that she ran to tell the other disciples, "I have seen Christ! Christ is alive!"

Christ is still alive. At this time of year the whole world reminds us that Christ is alive. The flowers and trees are coming back to life again. Butterflies come out of their grave-like cocoons and brighten the world with new life and beauty. [*Give each child a sticker or bookmark with a picture of a butterfly on it.*] When you follow Christ like Mary Magdalene did, Christ will make your life even more beautiful than a butterfly.

Prayer

Dear Christ, how excited we feel to know that you came back to life and that you are still alive today. We want to be your faithful followers, like Mary Magdalene. Come alive in our hearts today! Amen.

Activity Center

On work tables place bright-colored magic markers, water colors, butterfly stickers, construction paper of various colors, white paper, and pictures of Mary Magdalene and butterflies. Help the children in making Easter cards to take to people in nursing

NEW TESTAMENT ──────────────────────────── 75

homes. Encourage them to imagine Mary Magdalene's feelings when she saw the resurrected Christ for the first time and to draw or paint the pictures they see in their minds. Also let them use their imaginations in connecting pictures of the resurrection with butterflies. Talk about the risen Christ's living in the hearts of followers, like Mary Magdalene and Peter, as well as women and men today.

BIRTHDAY GIFTS (Acts 2:1–21)
[Pentecost]

[*Decorate the room with balloons.*] Today we are celebrating Pentecost Sunday. What do you know about Pentecost? [*Let the children respond.*] Pentecost is the birthday of the church. That's why the colorful balloons decorate this room. What do you like best about birthdays? [*Give each child a small gift, like a sticker or bookmark.*] When the church was born on Pentecost, God gave the people gifts.

[*Ask four or five of the children to take a hand puppet and help tell the story.*] We're going to make these puppets come to life and tell the story of Pentecost. Let's imagine that these puppets are the disciples gathered in a room in Jerusalem. Jesus had told them to wait there and pray for the Holy Spirit. So all the disciples folded their hands and bowed their heads in prayer. [*Help the children fold the hands and bow the heads of the puppets.*] Then all of a sudden they heard a loud sound! They looked up and saw flames coming down from heaven! [*Make the puppets jump up, spread their arms, and look up.*] Then the Holy Spirit filled the disciples, and they started talking in languages they had never even studied. [*Make the puppets look as though they are speaking.*] People from many different countries gathered when they heard the loud sound. These people spoke different languages. The disciples could use God's gift of speaking different languages so that these people could understand the Good News of Jesus' love. Then Peter preached, and three thousand people believed in Jesus. [*Have one of the puppets be Peter and pretend to preach.*]

[*Take the puppets off the children's hands.*] See how flat and lifeless these puppets are unless they are on your hands. The puppets came alive with your help. You have to put them on your hands for them to be what they were made to be. This is the way it is with the Holy Spirit's gifts to us. They will be flat and useless without our help. We have to use God's gifts so that they come alive. The disciples used the Holy Spirit's gift of speaking in different languages to tell people about Jesus and to help the church grow.

The Holy Spirit comes to us today and gives us gifts. Some of us may have the gift of singing, others of speaking, others of helping people, others of art, others of playing some musical instrument, others of writing. The Holy Spirit gives us different gifts so that the church can do many different things. When we use these gifts, they help the church to come alive and to grow. Since this is the birthday of the church, let's think about ways we can give our gifts to the church.

Prayer

[Ask the children to pray silently about how they can give their gifts to the church.]

Activity Center

Seat the children in a circle. Ask them to talk about different gifts of the Spirit. Invite the children to take turns acting out ways they can give their gifts to the church. The other children will try to guess what the actor is doing, as in the game of charades. Then celebrate the birthday of the church with a birthday cake and ice cream. On the cake place a candle to represent each century of the church's existence, and explain to the children the approximate age of the church.

OTHER STORIES
OF FAITH AND COURAGE

A WOMAN WHO CHANGED OUR COUNTRY

Way back two hundred years ago a little girl named Isabelle was born in the big city of New York. Her nickname was "Belle." Belle was born a slave. She was not free like you and me. People owned her and sold her whenever they pleased. When she was eleven years old, she was taken far away from her family and sold to a cruel master. She felt so sad and lonely. She missed her mother and daddy and brother Peter so much. Belle's mother had taught her that Jesus would always hear her and help her. So she cried out to Jesus, "It's not right for my master to treat me so cruelly. Help me, please, Jesus." Soon she was sold to a new master, who was kinder to her. But Belle still knew down in her heart that it was not right for her to be a slave. God wanted her to be free. So she prayed to be set free. Finally when she was a grown woman, God answered her prayer. She was freed.

Soon after she was freed, Belle was walking past a church one night. She heard the people talking and singing about the Jesus she loved and who had helped her so much. She wanted to go in, but she was afraid they would not let someone who had been a slave in the church. The next Sunday, Belle got up her courage and went to this church, and they did accept her as a member. In this church, Belle met a woman who cared enough about Belle and her son to pay for them to go to school. Belle now got the chance to develop her good mind and speaking talents.

Even though Belle was free, there were still slaves all over our country. Belle wanted to help these other slaves to freedom. But at first she was afraid of such a big, dangerous job. One day she felt God telling her to start travelling around our country and preaching to people to free the slaves. And she felt God giving her a new name. The new name was Sojourner Truth. "Sojourner" means someone who stays in a place just a short time and then moves on. She believed that God wanted her to preach in one place for a short time and then to move on to other places. She believed God gave her the last name "Truth," because God is Truth and she would be God's preacher. [*Show the picture of Sojourner Truth on page 78.*] Now Sojourner Truth felt brave enough to speak for God against the sin of slavery. She preached for the freedom of slaves and for equal rights for women. Sojourner preached that God made all people equal and that all should be free to become what God made them. Her love for God and for all people gave her courage to preach all around our country. She was brave enough to keep preaching her beliefs even when people called her bad names and threw tomatoes, eggs, and sometimes even rocks at her.

When she got up to preach, she often began with a song she had made up herself. It went,

> I am pleading that my people,
> may have their rights restored;
> for they have long been toiling,
> and yet have no reward.

Sojourner Truth's work for freedom paid off. Her preaching, along with a book she wrote, helped free the slaves. Sojourner Truth went to see Abraham Lincoln, who was the president of our country at that time. She thanked President Lincoln for all he had done to free the slaves. But Lincoln thanked Sojourner for all she had done to free the slaves. Lincoln told her that he had heard of her brave work long before he ever thought of being president. Lincoln thanked Sojourner for working so hard to change our country for the better.

You can be like Sojourner Truth. You can work to help people who are treated unfairly. With God's help, you can be brave like Sojourner Truth. You can do so much to change our country and our whole world for the better.

Prayer

Our God, we thank you for Sojourner Truth and all she did to change our country for the better. Help us also to be brave enough to do what's right. Help us to work for those changes that will make all people free to become what you want us to be. Amen.

Activity Center

On tables place used newspapers, used news magazines, scissors, paste, and poster or butcher paper. Invite each child to decide one change he or she would like to make in our country. Ask the children to cut out pictures to illustrate these changes and to paste these pictures on a large poster or sheet of butcher paper that has these words printed at the top: "Changing Our Country for the Better." Lead the children in a discussion of ways they can work together to make these changes.

LOVING THOSE WHO HURT US

Back in the 1950s, a little boy named Eric grew up in a small town in Texas. Eric's parents were ministers. They taught Eric that God loved him and that he was special to God. They encouraged Eric to work hard in school so that he could be his best for God. Eric was very smart. He loved school. He studied hard and made good grades. He lived only two blocks from one of the best schools in town. But he couldn't go to that school. He had to walk right past this school and keep walking for two miles to get to his school. Now that doesn't make any sense to walk two miles to a school when there's a good school just two blocks from your house, does it? The reason Eric couldn't go to the school close to his home was that he was black. Back then, only white children were allowed to go to that school.

The same thing happened to Eric when he got ready to go to high school. The best high school was close to his home, but he was not allowed to attend because he was black. He had to walk four miles to another high school. He didn't even get to ride a bus.

This was not the only unfair treatment Eric suffered. He couldn't even get into one of the movie theaters in town because he was black. He could sit only in the balcony of the other theaters to watch a movie. Eric was not allowed to drink from the same water fountains as white people. He had to drink from fountains marked "colored."

How would you feel if you were treated like Eric was treated?

The way he was treated was wrong. It was wrong in God's eyes for Eric to be treated this way, because Eric was created in God's image just like white children.

Some people who receive such bad treatment try to get even. But Eric didn't strike back. Instead he worked hard and did well in school. Then he went to college and then to seminary to get training to be a minister. With his excellent education and talents, Eric could have gone almost anywhere. But he decided to come back to his small hometown to try to show God's love and make things better. He came back as Rev. Eric Hooker and became pastor of one of the churches in his hometown.

By this time, some things were better. Because of the work of Dr. Martin Luther King, Jr., and many other caring people, black and white children could now go to school together. And everyone could get into all the movie theaters and sit wherever they wanted and could drink from any water fountain. But Rev.

Hooker saw that his hometown still had a long way to go. Black people were still treated unfairly. And this is still wrong. It is wrong for people to be treated unfairly because of the color of their skin. So Rev. Hooker got busy doing all he could to see that people are treated fairly and equally. He worked long, hard hours in his church and all over town to make things better for everyone.

I hope you'll be like Rev. Hooker and Dr. King. When you see people treated unfairly, God wants you to speak out and to work to change things.

Eric is like Joseph in the Bible. You remember that Joseph had plenty of reason to get even. His brothers sold him as a slave (Gen. 37–45). But Joseph reached out in love to those who had hurt him, just like Rev. Hooker continues to reach out in love, trying to change people who hurt him.

Prayer

God, our Friend, we're so glad that you love each one of us just the same. Help us to love one another and to treat one another fairly. Help us to love even those who hurt us. We believe that love can change unkind people. Thank you for always being our Friend who listens and understands. Amen.

Activity Center

On tables place paper, pens, colored markers, and colored pencils. Invite the children to write a story about an experience they had of helping someone who was treated unfairly. An alternative would be to write a story about something they would like to do to change unfair treatment of people. If they would like, the children could draw illustrations to go along with their stories. Some may prefer to draw pictures instead of write stories. Then bring the children together in a circle. Invite them to tell their stories to the group.

THE DREAM IS ALIVE

Does anyone want to "play like" with me? [*Show the children a spaceship made from Legos or some other kind of toy spaceship.*] Let's play like we're inside this Lego spaceship, on our way to the moon. [*Pass the spaceship around and let the children play like they're launching it.*] How do you think you would feel if you were soaring to the moon inside this spaceship? What would you want to do when you got to the moon? What are some other things you imagine yourself doing when you "play like"? It's fun to dream big dreams. Big dreams can help us work hard to make these dreams come true.

In Washington, D.C., there is a huge museum called the National Air and Space Museum. This museum has the *Kitty Hawk*, the first airplane, and many other famous airplanes and spaceships. Each one represents dreams come true. Everyday the museum plays a movie called *The Dream Is Alive*. The movie shows fantastic things being done in space that once were just wild dreams in someone's mind. People now walk not only on the moon, but out in space, outside the spaceship! The dream of conquering space is alive and coming true.

The dream of Sally Ride came true. Sally Ride is the first American woman astronaut. Sally held on to her dream to be a space woman even though people told her she couldn't, because she was a woman. But she studied hard and worked hard to prepare anyway. And she kept her dream alive in her mind. And now she is an astronaut.

God wants us to dream big dreams. God does great things in our world through people who have great big dreams. Sometimes we call this having faith. Jesus said that those people who have faith will be able to do the works that Jesus did and even greater works. "Truly, truly, I say to you, those who believe in me will also do the works that I do; and greater works than these will they do, because I go to God" (John 14:12). And Jesus did many things that people thought were impossible. God wants us to have big dreams of helping people and making this world better.

Prayer

We thank you, God, for Sally Ride and others who have kept their dreams alive and worked to make them come true. Help us to dream big dreams of making our world better for everyone. Amen.

Activity Center

Place Legos and other kinds of building blocks on tables or on the floor. Invite the children to build things that represent dreams they have for making the world better. Encourage them to talk with one another about these dreams.

ON MISSION FOR GOD

A woman named Maria Fearing lived back in the 1800s. Maria was born in 1838. She was born a slave in Gainesville, Alabama. When she was a child, she went to church with her owner. She heard stories about children in other countries who had never heard about Jesus. Her heart was especially touched by stories of children in Africa. So she promised herself, "I will go to Africa some day if I can."

Maria did not gain her freedom from slavery until she was almost thirty. She remembered her promise to go to Africa to tell people about Jesus. And she knew she needed an education to go as a missionary. So when she was thirty-three years old, she went back to school and completed the ninth grade. Then she taught in a small country school for a while. When she first applied to be a missionary, the mission board turned her down. The leaders told her that they would not send her because they thought she was not well enough educated and was too old.

But Maria felt so strongly that God wanted her to go to Africa that she would not take no for an answer. If the foreign mission board would not pay her way to Africa, she would raise enough money to pay her own way. She was a determined woman. First, she sold her house. Then she convinced her church to give her some money. With this money in hand, she went back to the mission board and asked to be allowed to pay her own way. They agreed, and Maria set out for Africa. Not until she was fifty-six did she get to go to Africa as a missionary. But she knew she was not too old.

After she had been in Africa for two years, the mission board decided to support her because she was doing such a wonderful job. She shared the love of Christ with many people. She took young girls who were about to be sold as slaves and built houses to keep them herself. She taught them and loved them. Because of her example, other missionaries built homes for children who had no homes. She stayed in Africa until she was eighty years old, and then the mission board asked her to retire. She didn't want to leave her work in Africa. But when she came back home to the United States, she continued to tell people about Jesus' love and show them Jesus' love. Maria Fearing was a missionary until she died at age ninety-nine.

Maria Fearing was a missionary in Africa and here in the United States. She was on mission for God as long as she lived. Do you think you can be a missionary right here where you live? In what ways can you be on mission for God in your school and home and neighborhood? You can tell people the Good News that Christ loves them and wants the best for them. [Read Acts 1:8.] And you can show people the love of Christ by helping people in need.

Prayer

Thank you, God, that Maria Fearing worked so hard to show people the Good News of your love. Help us also to be on mission for you in the name of Christ. Amen.

Activity Center

Seat the children in a semicircle around you. Invite the children to discuss ways they can be on mission for God. Show them pictures of various mission opportunities in your community. Tell them about mission projects other children's groups have undertaken. Examples include the following: (1) making cards or small gifts and taking them to nursing home residents or to children in hospitals; (2) saving money and taking it to the local Salvation Army or some other relief ministry; (3) going door to door and collecting canned goods for a local food pantry for needy people; (4) for older children, doing clean-up jobs at a Habitat for Humanity house under construction or some other housing project for the poor. Help the children to choose a project and to plan to carry it out.

BE SOMEBODY!

A long time ago, back in the sixteenth century, there lived a girl named Teresa. She grew up in a town called Avila in the country of Spain. Later she was called Teresa of Avila. When Teresa was only twelve years old, her mother died. Then her father sent her away to another city to go to school. Teresa felt very sad because she missed her mother and because she had to go away from home.

Sometimes when our feelings are badly hurt, we also get sick physically. For instance, we might feel really scared and then get an upset stomach. Does that ever happen to you? Teresa started having fainting spells and pains in her heart. One of her teachers, who was a nun, helped Teresa when she was sick. This teacher also encouraged Teresa to become a nun. Who knows what a nun is? [*Help the children with this definition and also help them to understand what a convent is.*]

Teresa became the kind of nun who stays in the convent all the time and prays most of the time. But Teresa was still not well. She had more and more fainting spells and heart pains. Sometimes she got so sick that she couldn't even move her arms and legs. She had an upset stomach every morning. She felt so bad that she couldn't pray for a while.

But one day she felt Christ come to her and give her new life. She felt Christ telling her to go out and help people. So she started traveling in a covered wagon. She traveled miles and miles even in the terrible heat and the icy cold weather. She taught people what she had discovered about God and about prayer. She started fifteen new religious convents. And she wrote four books about God. Some people didn't like what she was doing. They thought she should just stay in the convent and pray. She could have stayed in that convent where she was safe and secure. But because she did what God wanted her to do, she helped people and helped change the church for the better. She became a great writer. And she felt better than ever because she was doing something important with her life. As long as she stayed in the safe convent, she was weak and sickly. But when she went out to help people, she felt much better. She became *somebody* when she reached out to help others.

God has big plans for each one of you. How many of you want to do something really important? God made each of you to do something important, to be *somebody*. God doesn't want you to be satisfied with just getting by in your school work or with doing anything in a sloppy way. God wants you to be your very best. When you do what God wants, you will do something important like Teresa did. You will be *somebody*.

Prayer

God, teach us to help others so that we will do what's really important. Thank you for making each one of us to be *somebody*. We pray in the name of our Friend, Jesus. Amen.

Activity Center

Invite the children to play the game of charades. Seat the children in a circle, and let them take turns in acting out something they can do to help others or something they can do well. Ask each child to introduce the act with the words, "I am somebody because I can," and then pantomime the action. Tell the other children to guess the action and tell why this would make the child *somebody*. For example, a child might pantomime helping a teacher decorate the bulletin board in the classroom. This action would make the child *somebody* for many reasons: (1) the child uses special skills and talents to make the room more attractive; (2) the children learn from the bulletin board; (3) the child helps the teacher do a better job; (4) other children appreciate the work of the child; (5) the teacher praises the child for a job well done.

DREAM BIG!

Dream big. Whatever you're thinking of doing with your life, dream bigger.

Marie Curie lived from 1867 to 1934 in a country called Poland. When she was just five years old, she saw some glass test tubes and other scientific equipment in her father's workroom. She was fascinated and curious. She asked her father what these things were, and he told her, "physics apparatus." Even though she didn't understand what these words meant, she thought they sounded wonderful, so she turned them into a little song. She started dreaming about doing something with this physics apparatus. She dreamed of being a scientist when she grew up. A few years later, she went to a small private school for girls. But going to a small school didn't keep Marie from having big dreams.

When Marie was only nine, one of her older sisters died. Then the next year, her mother died. Losing two people she loved so dearly was very hard for Marie. It was hard growing up without a mother. But she held on to her dream of being a scientist, and she worked hard in school.

Marie did so well in school that she got to skip two grades. She scored at the top of her classes in math, English, history, German, French, and religion. She dreamed of going to a famous school in Paris, France. She dreamed of discovering some way to make life better for her people in Poland. When it came time for her to go to college, her father didn't have enough money to send her. But this didn't stop Marie from following her dream. She worked out a deal with her older sister. Marie agreed to work and earn money for her sister to study to become a doctor. Then her sister would help Marie go to college to become a scientist.

Finally it was Marie's turn to go to college. Even though her older sister, who was now a doctor, gave her some money, Marie still had a hard time paying for her expenses. She lived in a cold attic room and had only hot chocolate and black bread for many meals. But she was determined to be a scientist. Finally she earned a degree in physics and chemistry. Then she married a scientist. She and her husband began conducting scientific experiments in an old shed. Marie was determined to discover something to help people. Four years they worked hard day and night, mixing boiling chemicals, searching for a new element. Finally Marie Curie, also called Madame Curie, discovered a brand new element called radium. Radium is used to help people get well. It is used in X-rays and many other ways. Marie could have made a fortune on this new element, but instead she gave it to hospitals to be used in healing sick people.

Marie Curie received the Nobel Prize twice for her outstanding scientific work for the good of humanity. Marie followed her dream and would not give up even during very hard times.

She once said, "One must believe oneself gifted for something, and that something must be attained at whatever cost." Marie Curie not only accomplished her dream of discovering something that would help her own people in Poland, but also she discovered something that continues to help people all over the world.

You too can have big dreams. You may not be very big now, but you can dream big. God wants us to dream big. Jesus told the disciples to go to the whole world and tell people the Good News of God's love. Now that was thinking big. But Jesus promised them the power of the Holy Spirit to accomplish this big dream. The Holy Spirit still gives us power to use God's gifts to accomplish big dreams.

Prayer

God of every good and perfect gift, thank you for giving each one of us gifts. Help us to dream big so that we will use your gifts to the fullest. Thank you for Marie Curie and others who have helped people all over the world by accomplishing their big dreams. Amen.

Activity Center

On a flannel board, place figures (made of felt or flannel or paper with felt strips glued to the backs) to represent Marie Curie, her father, her sister, and her husband. Invite the children to use the flannel board to tell the story of Marie Curie and her big dream. Then invite them to tell about their big dreams.

A MISSIONARY DOCTOR

There is a doctor serving as a missionary in India today named Sharla. As long as Sharla can remember, she wanted to be a doctor. She always did well in school. Her parents encouraged her to work hard in school. Sharla went to school about twenty-five years in all, counting elementary school, high school, college, and medical school. It takes a lot of education to become a doctor. When Sharla graduated from medical school at the top of her class, her parents were very proud of her. Because Sharla had done so well in school, she was offered an excellent position at the hospital where she had done her training. This position was the head of internal medicine. Sharla would make a great deal of money if she took this job. And she would have a lot of power and respect as head doctor and teacher of internal medicine. Sharla also had offers to go into private practice and make even more money.

But Sharla turned down all these offers. For she had a dream in addition to being a doctor. She also wanted to be a missionary. She believed that God had called her to go take the love of Christ to another country. She believed that God could use her medical knowledge and skill to help needy people. Sharla heard about the desperate need for trained doctors in India. So she went to serve in a Christian hospital in Bangalore, India. Her parents had a hard time seeing her go. But they were proud of her for being willing to follow where God led her.

The conditions of the hospital in India were terrible compared to modern hospitals in our country. Sharla didn't have all the equipment and supplies she needed. And many of the people who came to her were dirty and had ugly sores on their skin because they didn't have enough food. There were so many sick people and so few doctors. Sharla had to work long hours every day. Sharla's friends back home had a hard time understanding why she would give up the chance to be an important doctor with a big salary in order to go far away from home to a country where she would get little recognition or money. Sharla serves God as a medical missionary in India because she believes this is what God wants her to do.

Sharla follows the example Christ gave us of serving others. Christ washed the feet of the disciples (John 13:1–15). They couldn't understand why Christ would do this job, because washing feet was the job of the lowest servant. But Christ teaches us that a great person serves others.

Prayer

We thank you for people like Sharla who follow Christ in serving people in need. Give us courage to do what you want us to do. Amen.

Activity Center

Place large bowls or pans of water, washcloths, and towels on tables. Invite the children to take turns washing one another's feet. Then bring the children into a circle and talk about what washing feet meant in Jesus' day. Lead them in discussing acts of service today that might be similar to washing feet (for example, helping sick or elderly people clean their homes or mow their lawns, cleaning their bathrooms at home, doing clean-up jobs at a Habitat for Humanity house under construction). Encourage each child to choose one of these acts of service.

MOTHERS OF OUR FAITH
[appropriate for Mother's Day]

Many women have done important work for God and the church. These women are mothers of our faith. I'm going to tell you about two of them. The first is Mary McLeod Bethune. [*Show her picture on page 93.*] Mary grew up the child of slave parents. Children of slaves did not have the opportunity to go to school and learn to read. Mary wanted to read more than anything. A church mission school gave her the chance to learn to read. She loved school. She worked hard and did very well in school. When she grew up, she decided to do something to help other children learn. She began a school in Florida for black workers' children. The school grew to become Bethune-Cookman College. Mary continued to work hard so that people could have equal opportunities. She was active in the Methodist church and helped to begin United Methodist Women, a group that supports mission work. She did so many good things for our country that she was chosen as an

OTHER STORIES OF FAITH AND COURAGE 93

advisor to four United States presidents. Mary once said, "God is the guide of all that I do."

The other woman I want to tell you about is Teresa of Calcutta. [*Show her picture above.*] Most people call her Mother Teresa. She is called "Mother," even though she has no children of her own. She is a mother to the many people she has cared for. Mother Teresa is a small woman who has done giant deeds for our world. In the country of India she has cared for people with leprosy, a disease that eats away the skin. Most people won't have anything to do with lepers, but Mother Teresa eases their wounds and tells them of God's love. She feeds hungry people in India and in many other parts of the world. She helps the poorest people in the world. She began the Society of the Missionaries of Charity. In 1979 she was honored with the Nobel Prize for Peace for her work in the struggle to overcome poverty in the world. Recently she has worked hard to help people who are sick with AIDS. Mother Teresa believes that we express our love to Christ by helping people.

Mary Bethune and Mother Teresa show us so much about God's love. These mothers of our faith show us that God loves everyone just the same. And God wants us to care for people who need our help. When we care for needy people, we are also caring for Christ. Christ said, "As you did it to one of the least of these my brothers and sisters, you did it to me" (Matt. 25:40).

Prayer

Help us to follow the example of Mary Bethune and Mother Teresa in caring for people in need, in the name of Christ. Amen.

Activity Center

On tables place stethoscopes (they can be toy stethoscopes), doctors' and nurses' "scrubs" (paper "scrubs" can be obtained free of charge from most hospitals or clinics), thermometers, school books, brief cases, clip boards, and other props that might be used to "play like" professionals in education and medicine. Invite the children to take turns pretending they are teachers, doctors, and nurses. Encourage each child to play each of the roles. Talk about how Mary McLeod Bethune and Mother Teresa helped people by providing education and health care. Invite the children to discuss ways they might want to help people.

WORKING TOGETHER

[*Have the children sit in a circle around a large chair. Ask a small child to move the chair. When he or she has trouble moving it, ask several others to help.*] It was easier to move the chair working together than working alone, wasn't it? Some things are just impossible for one person to do alone. And many things are so much easier to do if you have others to help you. Think of things that you do with the help of other people. [*Give time for the children to respond.*]

[*Wave a small American flag.*] Do you know who made the first American flag? Betsy Ross gets all the credit for making the first American flag. Betsy Ross is famous for this. But she didn't make the flag all by herself. There were many people who helped her with the design. There were other people who grew the cotton to make the cloth. There were still other people who made the thread she used to sew the flag. Betsy Ross didn't make the flag alone.

[*Show the children a telephone.*] Do you know who invented the telephone? Alexander Graham Bell gets all the credit for inventing the telephone. But Alexander Graham Bell did not invent the telephone alone. Many people had made important discoveries that helped him invent the telephone. Some discovered electricity. Others discovered the connection between electricity and magnets. And still other people discovered things about the sound of our voices and vibration. Alexander Graham Bell could not have invented the telephone alone. It took all these other people.

The first Christian church discovered that it was important for them to work together in order to grow. They shared their food and other things with one another. They worshipped God together. And they worked together to help people in need (Acts 2:44–47). It is important for us to work together to spread the Good News of Christ's love in every way we can. Just as it took more than one of you to move the chair, it takes more than one person to do the work of the church. It takes all of us working together to do the work of Christ.

Prayer

Loving God, show us how we can better work together to spread your love. We thank you for bringing us together in church so that we can do so much more than we could alone, in Christ's name. Amen.

Activity Center

On tables place construction paper, magic markers, used curriculum literature, scissors. Talk with the children about an idea you have for a bulletin board in a children's Sunday School room or in some other place in the church. Ask them to help in preparing materials for the bulletin board. Let the children know that working together makes the bulletin board much better than it would be if only one person prepared it. Talk about other ways we can work together in the church. Sing "All Children Together" (page 146).

SOMETHING BETTER

Billy lived with his mother, two older sisters, and one younger brother in a small house. Billy was nine years old and was just starting fourth grade. Billy looked around at his friends and felt that they had better clothes than he had. Some of his school supplies were left over from last year, and his friends had brand new crayons and folders. Billy had enough to eat and everything he really needed for school. But he felt bad that he didn't have all the things his friends had.

There was one thing that Billy really wanted that he didn't get. He wanted money to take to school to buy candy after lunch. Every day after lunch his friends would run to the candy machines and look at all the different kinds of candy and make their selections. But Billy didn't have any money. He felt so left out. He would just stand over in a corner and wait for them. Sometimes his friends weren't very nice. They would make him feel even worse by saying things like, "Hey, Billy, aren't you going to get any candy today?" They knew he never had any money. So why did they have to say this?

Over and over again Billy asked his mother for candy money. His mother would always say, "No, Billy. We just can't afford it. Besides the candy is not good for you." Billy tried to explain to his mother that it wasn't the candy that was so important to him. He just didn't want to feel so left out. He wanted to be able to join in the fun with his friends. But his mother still said, "No,

Billy." Billy begged, "Please, Mother, it's just thirty-five cents — just three dimes and a nickel." His mother didn't even answer him because she knew she couldn't make Billy understand why he couldn't have the money.

Billy decided he would try another way of asking for the money. He started leaving notes around the house, promising to clean his room or do some other work around the house. And at the end of the note there would be this sentence: "Mother, it would really be great if you would just surprise me by leaving thirty-five cents in my school bag." The next morning Billy would get up and slowly open his bag, hoping and praying that he would find thirty-five cents. But it was not there. And his mother never said anything about the notes.

A few months after school started, it came time for Billy's tenth birthday. He asked his mother if he could have his friends over for a party. All his mother said was, "No, Billy we can't afford it." Billy's heart sank. He went into his room and cried and cried. When his birthday came, he just tried to forget it. No one at home or at school even wished him "Happy Birthday." That afternoon he walked home from school feeling really lonely and sad. He unlocked the door, and to his surprise, there was a beautiful brand new bicycle. On the bicycle was a note:

> Happy Birthday, Billy. I've been saving up for this bicycle. That's why I couldn't afford candy money and some of the other things you asked for. I wanted you to have something really special on your tenth birthday. Love, Mother.

Billy had wanted a bicycle for a long time. But he had not even asked for one because he didn't think his mother could afford it. He had asked for dimes and nickels for candy, and his mother had given him a bicycle instead! And was he glad! He called his friends to come over and see his bike. He let them take turns riding his new bike. He had so much fun with his friends and his new bike.

Billy's mother said no to him because she had something better for him. God is often like this mother. We may ask God for something and not get it and wonder why. It may be because God has something better for us. One thing we know for sure. God loves us far more than any earthly mother or father and always wants the best for us.

Prayer

God, our Mother and Father and so much more than we can imagine, thank you for giving us what is best for us. Help us to remember when we don't get what we ask for that you have something better for us. Amen.

Activity Center

Seat the children in a semicircle around a flannel board or a blackboard. Ask for volunteers to use the flannel board or blackboard to tell the story of Billy and his mother and the bicycle. Ask for volunteers to tell about times when they didn't get what they asked for or prayed for but got something better instead. Talk about those times when they don't get something better. Help them to understand that God always works for our best, no matter what.

WHAT YOU DON'T KNOW WILL HURT YOU

Back during the second World War, there lived a boy named Jim. When he was a baby, Jim and his family moved from their home in England to China. The Japanese came over into China and started fighting the Chinese when Jim was ten years old.

One day the soldiers came into the city where Jim was living with his parents. The people in the city started trying to get out fast, so they wouldn't be killed by the bombing and shooting. Jim and his parents tried to leave in their car. But thousands of people crowded the streets. Their car couldn't get through, and shots were coming toward their car. So they jumped out into the crowd trying to run out of the city. They held hands tightly to stay together. But all of a sudden Jim dropped a toy plane, his favorite toy. When he reached down to pick it up, he turned loose of his mother's hand and got lost from them. Jim's parents looked and looked for Jim, but couldn't find him in the huge crowd of people. Jim tried to find his parents, but the crowd kept pushing him farther and farther away from them.

For the next few years Jim had a hard time without his parents. He struggled to make it on his own. He almost starved to death. Some American soldiers helped him by letting him stay with them and feeding him for awhile. Then Jim went with a group of people to a labor camp, where he had to work very hard and had little to eat. A kind doctor helped Jim continue with his school lessons. Jim got along well with everyone because he was friendly and helpful to people. Once he went outside the camp to try to catch a turkey for a special meal for his friends. The Japanese guard of the camp went looking for Jim. He sneaked up behind Jim and was about to shoot him. A Japanese boy about Jim's age saw the guard with his gun pointed at Jim. This Japanese boy named

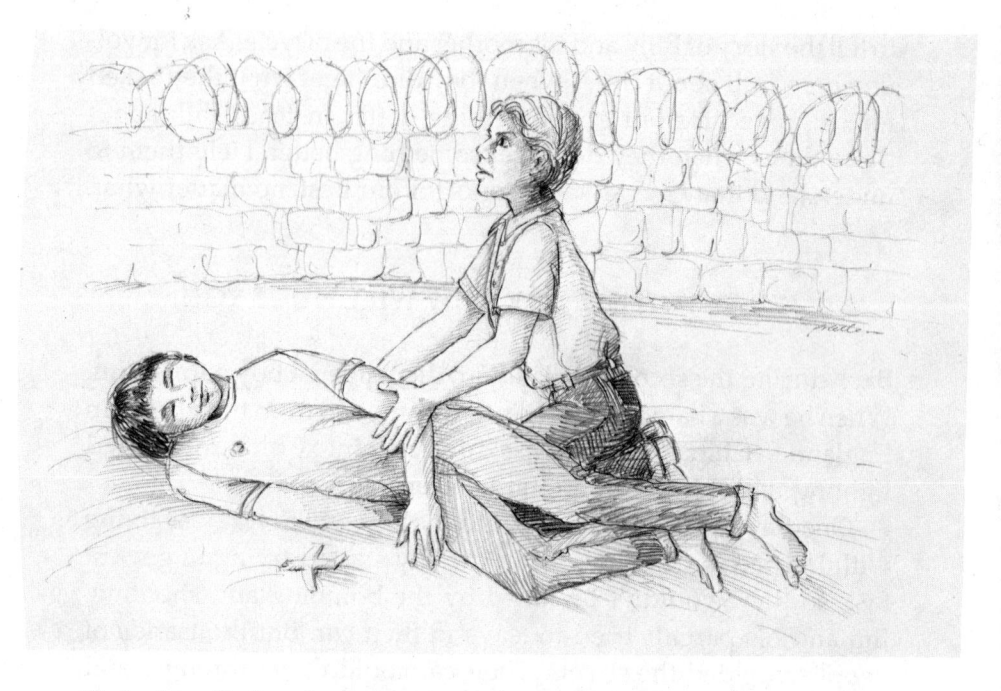

Tadashi called to the guard and got him off track. Jim was able to run to safety. Tadashi saved Jim's life.

Jim became good friends with Tadashi. They discovered that they both wanted to be pilots when they grew up. A while later Jim was out talking and having a good time with Tadashi. An American soldier who had helped Jim in the labor camp drove by in his jeep. He saw Jim and Tadashi, didn't understand what was going on, pulled out his gun, and shot Tadashi. Jim cried, "You killed my friend! You killed my friend! Didn't you know? He was my friend!" The soldier said, "He was Japanese. He was the enemy." Jim moaned, "But you didn't know him. He was my friend. He saved my life. If you had known him, you wouldn't have killed him."

One of the reasons people fight is that they don't really get to know one another. When we get to know someone who seems different from us, we find out that we are more alike than we thought. We become friends instead of enemies. Jesus wants us to learn "the things that make for peace" (Luke 19:42). One of the things that make peace is to get to know people and become friends with them. Jesus wants us all to be peacemakers.

Prayer

Help us to learn to be friends with others, even those who are different from us. Teach us to be peacemakers, O God. We thank you for always being our Friend. Amen.

Activity Center

Bring the children together with children from a congregation with a different racial majority or from a congregation of a different faith tradition, such as Jewish or Islamic. Divide the children into groups of four, with two from each congregation. Ask the children to talk with one another about their likes and dislikes and beliefs. Bring the children back together in a large group, and ask for volunteers to tell a little about a new friend they got to know. Lead the group in planning some future activity together, such as a party or a field trip.

GLORIA'S BIG GOAL

Not too many years ago a teenage girl named Gloria had a big goal. She wanted to be one of the star athletes in the Olympic contests. Gloria lived in the mountains of Montana, where it snows a good bit. When she was a little girl, Gloria started snow skiing. She loved to ski. A big event in the winter Olympics is cross country skiing. So she started working hard, exercising and skiing, training for the Olympics.

One day Gloria was out running in the mountains, preparing for the United States Olympic training camp. While she was jogging, she got shot in her shoulder. The bullet went all the way through her shoulder. She felt blood run down her back. She was hurt so badly that she could not make it back home by herself. She lay down out there waiting for someone to find her, hoping and praying that someone would come help her.

Finally after several days the rescue helicopter spotted her. By this time Gloria was just barely alive. She could hardly talk. The rescue workers took her as fast as they could go to the hospital.

When they got there, the doctors put Gloria in the intensive care unit. They didn't know if she could live. But slowly she began to get well. It took her a long time even to be able to get out of bed. She wondered how she would ever be able to ski again.

But Gloria had strong determination. She held on to her dream of being with the best athletes in the world in the Olympics. She was not about to give up her dream. But she knew that now she would have to work harder than ever to make her dream come true. She was a long way from being able to run and to ski. Every day she worked hard exercising. She got an exercise machine that helped her exercise the muscles in her arms and legs. Day after day, week after week, month after month, she exercised. It was hard work. And Gloria got very frustrated. But she kept working every day, going faster and faster on the exercise machine. Finally she was able to go out running in the mountains again. But she couldn't go far because she got tired quickly. And she got scared thinking about how she was shot when she was out running. But neither the fears she had inside nor her physical handicap stopped her. She kept right on trying. Soon she was able to ski again. Gloria continued to work and train, and she got stronger and stronger.

The time came for the Olympic try-outs. Gloria entered the cross country skiing event. It was a long, exhausting race. And it was a close race. Gloria won first place in that race, by just a few feet. Now she would get to compete in the Olympics, just as she had wanted to for so long. Her dream had come true. She was amazed that she was an even better athlete now than before her accident. Her family and friends were amazed. In spite of her accident and handicap, she became a winner.

All of us have handicaps or weaknesses that make it hard for us to achieve our goals. Maybe you want to play basketball, and you are not as tall as the other players. Maybe your family doesn't have as much money or as much education as someone else's. But with God's help you can still reach your goals.

The Apostle Paul had some kind of physical handicap. He asked God to take it away. But when God didn't take the handicap away, Paul went on about his work as a missionary. In fact, Paul became one of the greatest missionaries of all time. Paul said that God's power helps us when we are weak (2 Cor. 12:7–9). With determination and faith in God, you can reach your goals and make your dreams come true. God wants you to be the best you can possibly be.

Prayer

O God, help us to be like Gloria and Paul. Help us to keep on working toward our goals, no matter what. We thank you for giving us your power when we are weak. Amen.

Activity Center

On tables place poster paper, magic markers, crayons, scissors, paste, magazines, and newspapers. Ask the children to make posters of goals they want to achieve but wonder if they can because of some weakness or limitation. The children may draw their own pictures or cut pictures from magazines and newspapers and paste them on the poster. At the top of the posters, help the children write this verse: "My power is made perfect in weakness" (2 Cor. 12:9). Talk with the children about the meaning of this verse. Divide the children into pairs, and ask them to show each other their posters and talk about their feelings.

A GIRL WHO WOULDN'T GIVE UP

Mario and LaTasha decided to run for the office of president of their sixth grade class. Both were smart. LaTasha and Mario both had many friends. They got along well with everyone. Both had a good chance of winning the election.

The time came to start campaigning. Mario felt so sure that he would win that he didn't put much time into his campaign. LaTasha thought she had a good chance of winning. But she still worked hard on her campaign. She made posters to put up around the school. She called a bunch of her friends and asked them to come over and help her make posters. Wanting something creative that would catch the attention of students, she decided to put a sign on her horse that read, "Don't horse around. Vote for

LaTasha." She got permission from the principal to bring the horse to school and tie it to a post out on the playground. Then LaTasha started working on her campaign speech. She really wanted it to be good, so she asked her speech teacher to help her. LaTasha worked hard writing it all out, and then she practiced saying it to her parents.

The day came for the speeches and the voting. Mario got up and said just a few sentences. It was obvious that he hadn't even thought about his speech. Then LaTasha got up and gave her well-prepared speech. Several of her teachers told her how good it was. After the speeches, the students voted.

The next day the principal announced the results. Who do you think won? [*Let the children respond.*] Mario won. You can imagine how bad LaTasha felt. When she got home from school, she cried and cried. She yelled, "It's just not fair. I worked so hard. And Mario did nothing. I proved I would be best for the job. It's just not fair that Mario won." Her parents hugged her and said that she was right. It wasn't fair. She did deserve to win. Then they tried to explain to her that some things in life are just not fair.

And we can't always understand why these things happen. They told her that the important thing is how we deal with these unfair things. We can just stay mad and give up trying. Or we can keep trying to make things better for everyone. LaTasha's parents told her about how President Abraham Lincoln never gave up. He lost eight elections before he won the election to President of the United States.

LaTasha decided to be like President Lincoln and keep on trying. The next year she ran again for president of her class. Although she worked hard, she lost again. But she refused to give up. The next year she ran for vice-president and won. Then the following year she reached her goal of being president of her class. Because she wouldn't give up, LaTasha accomplished her goal of serving as president of her class.

There are probably things that have happened to each one of you that you think are not fair. It would be great if the best person or the best team always won. But many times the best person does not win. The important thing to remember is that we should keep trying even when unfair things happen. We can be like LaTasha in refusing to give up.

God told the prophet Habakkuk not to give up even though his people had been treated unfairly. God told Habakkuk that his vision of fairness would some day come true (Hab. 2:1–3). God will also help us to keep on trying to reach our goals.

Prayer

You know, God, that we get mad and hurt when we are treated unfairly. We believe that you care, and feel the same way about unfairness. We know that you never give up. Help us never to give up, but to keep trying to reach our goals so that we can make this world better. Amen.

Activity Center

Divide the children into groups of three or four. Ask the children to talk within their groups about times when they have been treated unfairly. Then have each group choose one situation and plan to role play that situation. Bring the children together in a large group. Ask the small groups to take turns presenting their role plays. Allow a little time after each role play for any of the children to express their feelings about the unfair situation they have watched.

FEELING FORGIVEN

The great day finally came! Her sixteenth birthday! For years Nicole had looked forward to the day she could get her driver's license. Several months before, she had passed Driver's Education. And then she studied for the written part of the driver's license test. On her birthday, Nicole got up bright and early and went to take the test. She passed the test! Now she had her driver's license and could drive. This was a big day for Nicole!

There was only one problem. Nicole had her new driver's license, but not much chance to drive. Nicole's mom and dad used their car most of the time in their work. So Nicole didn't get the car as much as she wanted. She didn't really need to drive to school and church, because she lived close enough to walk. But she wanted to drive just for fun. Nicole's parents finally let her take the family car out on weekends when they weren't using it.

One Saturday afternoon Nicole got the car to go to a friend's house. This was only the third time she had ever taken the family car out alone. And did she feel important! The car was brand new — a bright red Buick LeSabre. Nicole went cruising down main street in the big new car. She went the longest way, going by many of her friends' houses to honk and show off. She wasn't watching carefully enough where she was going and turned a corner too sharply. Crash! She hit a street sign! It was one of those signs we don't see much anymore — a big solid white post. Nicole was shocked and scared to death. She wasn't hurt, but she almost wished she had been. It might have been easier to face her parents. She knew from the sound and the force of the impact that she had really hurt the car. Slowly she made herself get out of the car and look at the damage. It was bad, even worse than she thought.

OTHER STORIES OF FAITH AND COURAGE

The whole right side of the car was caved in. The right front door wouldn't even open. "Oh, how am I going to face my parents?" she moaned. "I've wrecked their new car. They'll never forgive me. They'll never trust me again."

On the way back home, Nicole tried to think of something she could do, some way she could pay for the repairs. She remembered her savings bonds. For about six years she had been saving money for college. She could cash her bonds and pay for the repairs. So she rushed in the house and started going through her desk drawers looking for her savings bonds. Her mother came in and asked Nicole what was wrong. Nicole cried as she told her mother what had happened. She hugged Nicole and said that she was so glad that Nicole wasn't hurt. Her mother told Nicole that she forgave her. Then her dad walked in, and Nicole had to tell him. Nicole could see that he was upset about the car, but he said he forgave her too. They decided they would let her work to pay for the repairs, but they wouldn't take her savings bonds. Nicole felt so relieved that her parents had forgiven her. She promised to drive carefully from then on. She felt so grateful for their forgiveness.

God's forgiveness feels even better than our parents' forgiveness. When you've done something that you know is wrong, how do you feel inside? [*Allow time for the children to respond.*] God cares very much for us and will forgive us no matter what we have done. When God forgives us, we don't want to do that wrong thing again. We feel so grateful to God that we want to do better. The Bible tells us that God forgives our sins and helps us to be better people: "If we confess our sins, God is faithful and just, and will forgive our sins and cleanse us from all unrighteousness" (1 John 1:9).

Prayer

Loving and Forgiving God, we thank you that you are always there to love and forgive us. We come to you now, each one of us asking you to forgive us for the wrong things we have done and for the things we did not do that we should have done. [*Pause for silent prayer. Invite the children to tell God silently what they have done or not done and to ask for forgiveness.*] Thank you for forgiving us. Amen.

Activity Center

Seat the children around tables and ask them to be perfectly silent. Invite them to write down or draw pictures of several things they have done that were wrong or things that they should have done that they did not do. Ask them not to tell or show anyone what they have written. Then ask them to fold their pieces of paper and place them in a Pyrex container that you pass around. Burn the pieces of paper. Explain to the children that you have just given them a picture of God's forgiveness. God doesn't keep our sins and hold them against us. When we ask for forgiveness, God gets rid of our sins.

PAMELA PEACEMAKER

There once was a girl named Pamela, who lived in a home where there was much arguing and complaining. Pamela didn't like all the fighting, but somehow she would get caught up in it all. At school she noticed that many of the children, and even some of the teachers, couldn't get along with one another. Pamela loved to read. She read about people all over the world having trouble getting along with one another. Some even fought wars over their disagreements. It seemed that everywhere Pamela looked, and in everything she read, people were fighting. Finally Pamela had enough. She decided that she would try to be different and try to change some of the people around her.

One day she saw two of her friends out in the vacant lot between their houses. They were arguing about where they would go to play. They were both tired of their own houses and wanted to go to the other's house. One said, "Let's go to your house."

The other said, "No, I want to go to your house."

"But it's my turn to go to your house!"

"Is not! It's my turn."

On and on it went like this. Finally Pamela stepped in and said,

OTHER STORIES OF FAITH AND COURAGE — 109

"Hey, wait a minute. You could have been having fun playing all this time you've been standing out here arguing. Why don't you just come to my house and play?" So they went, and everyone had a good time.

The next day Pamela's older brother started trying to aggravate her, as he often did. He said, "You stupid head. You really get on my nerves. Why don't you just get out of here?" The first thing that came to Pamela's mind to say was, "Well, I was here first. You get out. You're the stupid one." But she didn't say this. She had learned something very important: it takes two to fight. So she said to her brother, "I didn't like what you said. It made me feel angry. But I still love you." This caught her brother off guard. He didn't have anything to say back. Pamela had chosen not to get into a fight with him.

Over and over again Pamela helped stop fights. Her changed

attitude helped change the attitudes of those around her. Soon she got the nickname, "Pamela Peacemaker." She felt much happier making peace than getting into fights. And she made many people happier.

God wants us all to be peacemakers wherever we are. In the famous Sermon on the Mount, Jesus said, "Blessed are the peacemakers, for they shall be called children of God" (Matt. 5:9). The word "blessed" means "happy." When we become peacemakers, we will be happy, just like Pamela. Let's say this verse together. "Blessed are the peacemakers, for they shall be called the children of God." [*Repeat the verse several times.*]

Prayer

Dear God, we want to be your happy children and to make our world happier. Help us then to be peacemakers, in the name of Jesus, the greatest peacemaker who ever lived. Amen.

Activity Center

Give each child a dove pin, a dove sticker, or a bookmark with a dove on it. Explain that the dove is a symbol for peace and for the Holy Spirit who helps us to live in peace and to bring peace to our world. Tell them that this dove will remind them that they can be peacemakers just like Pamela.

Ask the children to take turns acting out the role of peacemaker as several other children act out the scenes in the story of Pamela and other situations they have seen at home and school. Encourage the children to use their imaginations in creating solutions to the conflicts.

A BOY WHO CONQUERED FEAR

There is a musical drama called *The King and I*. Some of you may have seen the movie version of it. A mother and her son were launching out on a totally new experience. The boy was about ten years old. His dad had died several years before. His mother accepted a job as a teacher of the children of the King of Siam. This king had about twenty children.

The hardest part about this new job was that it was in a country far away from the home of the mother and son. They had to travel a long time on a ship to get from their home in England to Siam, which today is called Thailand. When they were almost there, the boy told his mother how scared he was to be going to a new country where he didn't know anyone. The people in this new country looked different from him and ate different foods and had different ways of doing things. He didn't know if he would like living in Siam. And he was afraid the people would think he was strange and wouldn't like him. His mother told him that she understood how he was feeling, because she felt scared too. But she told him something he could do that would help him feel better. When that feeling of fear would come up inside him, he could start whistling a happy tune. He could get the fear out of his heart by replacing it with a happy tune.

When they arrived in Siam, the boy and his mother stepped off the ship and into the new country. All around them were people who looked different from them and who spoke a different language. Everything seemed so strange. The boy felt fear flood his heart. He choked back the tears. Then he looked at his mother, and she started whistling. He began to whistle too — at first softly and weakly, but then louder and louder. As he whistled, he began to feel strong and brave enough to begin his life in a new country. The boy conquered his fear and launched out into this new country.

Do any of you ever feel afraid? All of us feel scared at times. What do you do to help you when you feel afraid? The boy in *The King and I* whistled a happy tune. The Bible gives us an even better way to deal with fear. In the book of Psalms we learn that trusting in God helps us when we feel afraid: "When I am afraid, I put my trust in thee" (Ps. 56:3). [*Have the children repeat this verse until they know it by memory.*] Let's ask God to help us with our fears.

Prayer

Understanding God, we thank you for understanding all our feelings. You know there are times when we feel afraid. Help us to trust you when we feel afraid. Amen.

Activity Center

On tables place drawing paper, pencils, crayons, magic markers, scissors, paste, magazines, and newspapers. Ask the children to draw pictures or make collages of things that make them afraid. At the bottom of their art work, ask them to write the verse: "When I am afraid, I put my trust in thee" (Ps. 56:3).

Sit on the floor or a low chair and gather the children close around you. Encourage the children to show their art work and talk about times when they feel afraid. Through your words, facial expressions, and body language, try to show the children God's understanding and concern. Use touch and hugging, with sensitivity to children's individual needs.

DOING THE IMPOSSIBLE

There's a verse in the Bible that we need to learn: "With God all things are possible" (Matt. 19:26). Let's say this verse together until we know it from memory. [*Repeat the verse several times together, and then ask for volunteers to say the verse by themselves.*] A girl named Rhonda shows us what can happen when we really believe this verse. When she was a young girl, she had polio. Almost never does anyone get polio anymore, because we now have polio vaccine. But Rhonda got polio before the vaccine was available to everyone. Rhonda had such a bad case of polio that she became paralyzed from her neck down. That means she couldn't move her arms and hands and legs. She couldn't walk. She couldn't even breathe by herself. Most of the day she had to stay in an iron lung. An iron lung looks like a big box that covered her whole body with only her head sticking out. [*Show her picture on page 113.*] The iron lung breathed for her. Now we wouldn't think that somebody in this shape would ever be able to do anything. Many people would just give up and not even try. But not Rhonda!

Rhonda's mind remained sharp and healthy. So she wanted to stay in school. Her parents got teachers to come to their home. Even though Rhonda was smart, she had a hard time doing school work. Imagine how it would be if you couldn't use your hands to hold a book or to write. But Rhonda wouldn't give up. She believed God wanted her to learn, so she trusted God to help her. Rhonda learned to hold a pencil in her mouth and write. [*Try to demonstrate this.*] Her parents set up a stand for her to put a book on and made a device for her to put in her mouth to turn pages in the book. Later Rhonda learned to type with a device in her mouth. Rhonda did well all through elementary, junior high, and high school.

But that's not all! Rhonda believed that God wanted her to go to college and would help her go. Many people thought this was impossible. But Rhonda believed that with God's help it would be possible for her to go to college. With a great deal of hard work, she learned to breathe outside her iron lung by sucking in air through a tube. She had friends who pushed her in a wheel chair from class to class. She was able to take tests and write papers with her special typewriter that she operated with her mouth. All this took tremendous effort and faith in God. It took her longer to finish college than most students because she could take only a few courses each semester. But she just wouldn't give up. She strongly believed that God would help her conquer all these obstacles and finish college. One day she did graduate from college with a degree in journalism. And what a great day that was! Her parents and teachers and friends were so proud of her! But Rhonda didn't quit then.

Today Rhonda writes Sunday School lessons, articles for church magazines and newsletters, and books. Even though Rhonda doesn't look as though she would be able to do anything, she has achieved more than most people. She does amazing things because she uses what she has — her good mind — and works hard and trusts God to help her. She refuses to let anything stand in her way. Rhonda learned that "with God all things are possible."

God wants us all to do the best we can with what we have. We too can do amazing things if we use what God has given us and trust God to help us. Remember that "with God all things are possible." [*Repeat the verse together.*]

Prayer

We thank you for Rhonda and other people who show us that with your help we can do what seems impossible. God, may we learn to trust you more and to use the gifts you have given us. Amen.

Activity Center

On tables place pencils and paper. Ask each child to hold a pencil in her or his mouth and try writing or drawing with it. Suggest that the children try to write the verse: "with God all things are possible." Then ask each child to write or draw, with pencil in hand, something he or she would like to do that seems impossible. While the children are working, go from table to table, encouraging them to keep trying to do these things that seem impossible.

HELP COMES
[*Advent*]

Several years ago two boys were traveling with their mother from Texas to Louisiana. The older boy, named Lester, was ten, and the younger boy, named Anthony, was six. Early that morning their grandmother had called that their granddaddy had suddenly become very sick. This was their daddy's dad. Their daddy took the first plane out of town that morning to be with his dad. Lester and Anthony and their mother were planning to go that weekend. But that afternoon their daddy called and told them that their granddaddy had died. So late that afternoon Lester and Anthony and their mother started driving to Louisiana. The boys were upset that their granddaddy had died. Their mother felt very sad too.

When we get upset, sometimes we don't think as clearly as when we feel good. The mother forgot to fill the car with gas before they left that afternoon. And even though she knew the road to the small town in Louisiana well, she took a wrong turn. By this time it was getting late. There they were, out on a deserted road about ten o'clock at night, almost out of gas. They were lost. She started feeling panicky inside. But she knew she had to stay calm on the outside, because Lester and Anthony were already so upset about losing their granddaddy. But Lester soon began to catch on that something was wrong. The mother started praying silently that God would somehow help her find a gas station and get back on the right road. Soon they came to an old, run-down building. It looked as if it had once been a store, but it was now dark inside. Then all of a sudden they saw a woman standing outside. They had not seen her coming out of the building or walking along the road. They didn't know what she was doing out there so late at night. She just all of a sudden seemed to appear. They stopped and asked her where the nearest service station was. She gave them directions. It was not too far. They got to the station, filled the car, and got back on the right road. When they knew they were safe, Lester said, "Mom, I think that woman who gave us directions was an angel sent by God to help us." His mother agreed and told the boys about her prayer for help.

The Bible says that God may come in the form of angels to help us. "And God will give angels charge of you to guard you in all your ways. On their hands they will bear you up, lest you dash your foot against a stone" (Ps. 91:11–12). God came to help Anthony, Lester, and their mother that night in the form of the woman who gave them directions.

Sometimes when we're having hard times, we find God even more than when everything is going fine. Maybe you have lost a grandfather or grandmother or someone else you loved. Or maybe you have had other times when you felt very sad, and God came to you in a special way. At this time of year we celebrate God's coming into the world in the form of Christ. During this Advent season, we want to invite Christ to come into our lives.

Prayer

We thank you that you come to us in so many ways. We invite you, Christ, to come into our lives at this special time of year and always. Amen.

Activity Center

Ask the children to get comfortable in their chairs or to lie down on the floor. Have them close their eyes while you guide them in meditation. Have the children breathe slowly and deeply for several minutes. Then lead them in visualizing some time when they felt sad or scared or upset in any way. Guide them to imagine Christ coming to them, sitting down beside them, and talking with them. What do they want to say to Christ? What do they want Christ to say to them? Slowly lead the children out of the guided meditation to a discussion of their feelings during the meditation. Remind them that they can invite Christ to come to them any time they need help. Close by singing "Into My Heart" (page 152).

CHRISTMAS GOES ON
[*Christmastide*]

A little girl named Maria and her older brother, Alex, grew up in a small town in Mississippi. It seldom snowed in this Southern town. Maria and Alex had never even seen snow, except in pictures. How they longed for snow on Christmas or anytime. They loved to go to their neighbors' house and see their sled. These neighbors had moved from the North, where it snowed every winter. They told stories of all the fun they had sledding and skiing in the snow.

One morning in January, Maria and Alex woke up and looked out the window. They couldn't believe their eyes! Snow covered everything. It was beautiful, just like a fairyland. They were so excited! Classes were dismissed at school, because the buses couldn't get through on the icy roads. The neighbors came by on their sled and invited Maria and Alex to play in the snow with them.

But there was one problem. Alex had the flu. The doctor had said that he couldn't go out as long as he had fever. And he certainly couldn't play with other children because he would give them the flu. Alex was so upset. The first snow in his whole life — and he couldn't go out and enjoy it. Maria felt bad about going out when Alex had to stay in, but he told her to go on. He didn't want to spoil her fun too. For two days Alex looked out the window by his bed and watched Maria and the neighbor children sliding down the driveway on the sled. Sadly he also watched the sun come out and slowly melt the snow. He was afraid the snow would be all gone before he was well enough to go out.

The third morning Alex woke up free of fever. Finally he could go out and have fun in the snow. But he looked out the window and saw no snow in the driveway. All he could see were patches in the yard. Alex started crying because he thought he had completely missed the snow. The fun was all over, and he had missed it. But then he heard one of the neighbor children knocking on the door and yelling, "Alex, come on, quickly!" There's still some snow in the vacant lot across from our house." Alex and Maria and the neighbor children ran to the lot and found a hill still covered with snow. All day long they slid down the hill on the sled and played in the snow. Alex had not missed the snow after all. And they were so happy.

Some people feel sad after Christmas is over. Maybe they feel that they have missed something or someone they wanted to see. Or maybe they have had an exciting time and don't want it to end. But Christmas is different from the snow in Mississippi. Christmas doesn't melt away. In fact, it never really has to end. We put up the bright decorations and go back to school and work, but the best part of Christmas goes on and on. The best part of Christmas is God's gift to us. God gave us Jesus Christ to love us and to show us how to love. The shepherds went home after the first Christmas, still praising God for this wonderful gift. "And the shepherds returned, glorifying and praising God for all they had heard and seen, as it had been told them" (Luke 2:20). We too can keep on celebrating Christmas. Christmas never ends. Christmas goes on and on.

Prayer

We thank you, God, for your wonderful gift on Christmas. We praise you that Christmas goes on and on, because Christ's love goes on and on. Amen.

Activity Center

On tables place construction paper, drawing paper, colored pencils, magic markers, scissors, paste, play dough, magazines, and newspapers. Encourage the children to use their imaginations and these materials to represent parts of Christmas that last. For example, they might make collages of people giving gifts to one another or to needy people, or make play dough doves to represent the peace of Christ that lives on in our hearts.

PRAYERS FOR ALL FEELINGS

WHEN WE FEEL AFRAID

Mother God, I'm scared tonight,
Will You come hold me?
I always feel so safe with You.
Rock me in Your strong arms.
Sing to me of bright flowers and warm sunshine.
Hold me through this cold night. Amen.

*

Strong God, we have to stand before the class tomorrow and
    give reports.
You know how shy we are.
You know how scared we feel.
You know how afraid we are that we will make mistakes,
and the others will laugh,
and the teacher won't like us.
Please help us, God, to do our best,
because we've worked so hard.
Please be with us tomorrow, God,
when we stand before the class. Amen.

*

LEADER	We cry to God, who hears and answers us.
GROUP I	Now we can lie down and sleep, for God is with us.
GROUP II	We are not afraid of anything or anyone.
ALL	God hears us and helps us. Thank You, God, for blessing us. Amen.

(based on Psalm 3:5–8)

WHEN WE FEEL LONELY

Our Father, are You always there?
Sometimes we just wonder.
You seem so far away.
Whisper that You love us.
Hug us gently in Your arms.
Amen.

*

I feel so alone, God. Sometimes my mother seems too busy for me. And I don't even know where my father is. Sometimes my friends leave me out. And I feel so lonely. I just want someone to play with, someone to talk with, someone to care. Will You be my Mother and my Father and my Best Friend? I need You, God. Amen.

WHEN WE FEEL THANKFUL

FIRST READER	Today I saw a bright red rose, laughing and dancing in the breeze.
ALL	Thank You, God, for eyes to see bright red roses.
SECOND READER	Today I heard a bird sing a happy song. It made me feel like skipping along.
ALL	Thank You, God, for ears to hear happy, skipping bird songs.

PRAYER FOR ALL FEELINGS

THIRD READER	Today I felt the soft, smooth fur of a black puppy. It made me feel cozy and warm all over.
ALL	Thank You, God, for hands to feel soft puppy fur.
FOURTH READER	Today I tasted a sweet, yummy chocolate chip cookie.
ALL	Thank You, God, for tongues to taste yummy chocolate chip cookies.
FIFTH READER	Today I smelled new-mowed grass. It made me feel fresh and clean all over.
ALL	Thank You, God, for noses to smell fresh-mowed grass.

*

I thank You, God, because You have saved me
and kept the students from making fun of me.
I asked You for help, my God,
and You came to me.
You helped me when I felt discouraged and upset.
You brought back good feelings.
You turned my tears into joy.
Thank You, God, my best friend.

(based on Psalm 30:1–5)

*

LEADER	You really are a good friend, God.
FIRST READER	You cried with me when my dog died, and when my best friend moved.
ALL	You really are a good friend, God.
SECOND READER	Your heart laughed and sang with mine when I made the honor roll, and when I hit a home run.
ALL	You really are a good friend, God.

*

Our God, it is good to give You thanks,
to sing praises to Your name, Almighty God;
to speak of Your love in the morning
and Your care every night,
with our prayers and songs we praise You.
You fill us with gladness.
Our God, we give You thanks.

(based on Psalm 92:1–4)

WHEN WE FEEL ANGRY

I am so mad, God! My parents won't let me do anything! My friends get to spend the night together, but my parents say I'm not old enough. They're always saying, "Wait till you get a little older." I feel that I'm missing all the fun. It makes me so mad that they treat me like a baby! I wish my parents let me do more. I wish my parents were like my friends' parents. Can You understand how I feel, God? I hope so, because You are the only one. Amen.

*

God, can You hear me?
Do you care how I feel?
Nobody else does!
It's just not fair!
I worked so hard.
Why did I make a bad grade?
The teacher said I didn't study.
But I know I did.
The test was just not fair!
My parents didn't believe me either.
Do you believe me?
I hope so. I believe so.
I believe You're on my side.
I believe You're my Friend.
Thank You, God.

*

PRAYER FOR ALL FEELINGS

LEADER	God, we look around us and see so many things that are just not right.
FIRST READER	It's not right for some people to go hungry.
SECOND READER	It's not fair for children not to have a decent place to live.
THIRD READER	It's not right for people not to have good jobs just because of their color or their sex.
FOURTH READER	It's not right for people to fight.
ALL	All this unfairness makes us angry. Do You care? Can You do something about it? Sometimes we feel angry with You when things don't change.
LEADER	Caring God, we know You are on the side of the weak and poor. You want to use us to help them. May we trust You and do our part to make things better. Amen.

*

O God, do something about those people who hurt us.
Beat up all those who make fun of us!
Stand up for us, because You know we're right.
Knock down those who're always out to get us.
Show them they're not so great as they think they are.
Blow them off their high horse.
For no reason they have been ugly and unfair to us.
God, how much longer will You let them get by with this meanness?
You see what they're doing.
Don't just stand by and watch.
Do something!
Take our side.
You are always fair, so bring fairness to us.
Don't let them get by with treating us cruelly.
Come help us, and we will praise You for Your goodness.
    Amen.

(based on Psalm 35)

WHEN WE FEEL SAD

Have You heard the bad news, God?
My grandmother just died.
   You know how much I love her.
   We baked cookies together,
   and went swimming and horseback riding.
    On warm summer days we had picnics in the park,
      And sat out under the cool, shady trees and talked
      and planned more good times together.
But now there won't be any more good times together,
   because my grandmother just died.
   I miss her so much already.
Can you understand how much I miss her?
Please help to fill the empty places in my heart, God.
Remind me that Grandmother is now happy,
having good times together with You. Amen.

*

   Our hearts are sad, O God.
   We cry during the day and at night.
   We long for You to comfort us.
   Our hearts are so sad;
      they ache and sigh.
   But You bring us comfort and loving kindness
      by day and by night.
   Our hope is in You,
      our Savior and our God. Amen.

(based on Psalm 42)

*

LEADER	God comforts us as a Mother comforts her children (Isa. 66:13).
GROUP	When we have to move away from our friends, we feel so sad, God.
LEADER	God comforts us as a Mother comforts her children.

PRAYER FOR ALL FEELINGS ———————————— 127

GROUP	When someone we love has to go away for a while, we feel so sad, God.
LEADER	God comforts us as a Mother comforts her children.
GROUP	When someone we love dies, our hearts hurt so badly, God.
LEADER	God comforts us as a Mother comforts her children.
GROUP	When our pets die, we feel so sad, God.
LEADER	God comforts us as a Mother comforts her children.
ALL	Hear our feelings, God, and come to us; comfort us as a Mother comforts her children.

WHEN WE FEEL HAPPY

We shout for joy to You, our God!
We want to serve You with happy hearts!
We come to You with songs of joy!
For You made us, and we know how special we are to You.
It makes us happy to know that You care so much for us.
We thank you and praise your name!
For you are good.
No matter what happens, You will always love us.

(based on Psalm 100)

*

LEADER	Your joy, O God, is our strength (Neh. 8:10).
GROUP	We feel so happy playing with our good friends, God.
LEADER	Your joy, O God, is our strength.
GROUP	Our families' love makes our hearts glad.
LEADER	Your joy, O God, is our strength.

GROUP	We feel good when we do our best in school.
LEADER	Your joy, O God, is our strength.
GROUP	We feel happy when we make someone else happy.
LEADER	Your joy, O God, is our strength.
GROUP	Our hearts dance for joy when we see bright flowers and golden sunsets and all things beautiful.
LEADER	Your joy, O God, is our strength.
GROUP	Our hearts sing for joy whenever we feel Your love.
ALL	Your joy, O God, is our strength.

*

FIRST READER	Today I made a new friend, and I feel so glad.
ALL	Thank You, God, for happy times with friends.
SECOND READER	The teacher says my work is good, and I feel so happy.
ALL	Thank You, God, for good times at school.
THIRD READER	My family now gets along better, and we all feel happy.
ALL	Thank You, God, for happy times with family.
FOURTH READER	Singing and playing with friends at church makes me feel so happy.
ALL	Thank You, God, for happy times at church.
FOURTH READER	My poem won first place, and I feel so proud and happy.
ALL	Thank You, God, for the joy of creating.
FIFTH READER	Today I saw a beautiful, bright-winged butterfly, and I smiled all over.
ALL	Thank You, God for the joy of your creation.

WHEN WE FEEL GUILTY

We know we disappoint You, Mother God.
We know we hurt You, Father God.
We know we make You feel sad, Christ, our Friend.
When we goof off at school, we disappoint You.
When we hurt others, we hurt You.
When we disobey our parents, You feel sad.
We're sorry, God.
Thank you for forgiving us. Amen.

*

Forgive us, Loving God,
    wipe away all our mistakes.
Help us to feel good and clean again.
For we know we have done wrong,
    and we feel bad.
We know we have hurt You,
    by doing wrong and not doing right.
Make our hearts pure and clean again,
    and help us to feel you with us once more.
May we feel joyful again,
    knowing that you forgive us.
Give us strength to do right,
    and to teach others the right way.
We thank you, and praise you
    for always loving us and forgiving us. Amen.

(based on Psalm 51)

*

We're sorry for the times we've been mean to people.
We're sorry for the times we've seen someone hurting,
    and pretended not to notice.
We're sorry for the times we've made fun of people,
    just because they're different from us.
We're sorry for the times we've left others out,
    and hurt their feelings.

We're sorry for the times we've said hateful things to others,
    and made them cry.
We're sorry for the times we knew someone needed a friend,
    and we walked away.
We're sorry for all these times we haven't loved enough,
    and hurt You.
Forgive us, God, and help us to love more
    as You love us. Amen.

WHEN WE'RE HAVING FUN

LEADER	Come play with us, God.
FIRST READER	We're planning a party,
SECOND READER	With games and presents,
THIRD READER	And lots of ice cream and cake,
FOURTH READER	And candy and prizes,
FIFTH READER	And maybe even a funny movie.
ALL	We're going to have so much fun! Come play with us, God.

*

We're planning a big trip, God, and we're so excited!
We've looked forward to this trip for a long time.
It's exciting just to think of all the fun times we will have.
Come go with us. It will be much better if you do.
You're our Friend, and we want you to go too. Amen.

*

How wonderful it is, God, to praise You at church.
We laugh and sing and dance and play with You,
    for You are so good to us.
We rejoice in Your wonderful creation
    that brings us joy and delight.

We have such a good time together
 with one another and with You.
We praise you with songs and dance
 and tambourines and cymbals.
You make life so wonderful, and we praise You!
Along with all creation, we praise You!

(based on Psalm 150)

SONGS OF JOY

SONGS OF JOY — 135

GOD IS

God is clo-ser than a bro-ther, Strong and gen-tle as a mo-ther;
God is warm like sum-mer sun-light, Bright as stars that shine on clear nights;
God is with us, God is in us, God is love.
God will lead us like a shep-herd, Stand be-side us like a friend would;
God is like the clouds a-bove us And the sol-id ground be-neath us;
God is with us, God is in us, God is love.

Deborah Harris, 1992
Words © 1992 Deborah Harris

Mark Hayes, 1992
Music © 1992 Mark Hayes

136   SONGS OF JOY

love.
love. God is the hope and kind-ness in our hearts;
God is the peace and pow-er in our minds; God is the joy of
ev-'ry girl and boy; God is with us, God is in us,
God is love.

SONGS OF JOY — 137

A PSALM OF UNITY
(based on Psalm 133:1)

Behold how good and how pleasant it is for brothers and sisters to dwell as one. Behold how good and how pleasant it is to share the Creator's love.

Words & Music ©1992 Deborah Harris

Arr. © 1992 Luther Mitchell, Jr.

SONGS OF JOY — 139

CHILD IN THE MANGER

Unison

Child in the man-ger, Child full of sor-row, out-cast and
Child in the man-ger, help us to learn to wel-come the

stran - ger, bear-ing dis - grace. Can our sal - va - tion rest in your
stran - ger, ho - ly em - brace. Love those who wrong us, serve those who

suf - fering? Hope of cre - a - tion in this low place.
scorn us, Christ Child a - mong us, bring us to grace.

Words ©1992 Sally Browder

Tune BUNESSAN, Gaelic Melody

MIRIAM'S TAMBOURINE

Mir-iam helped her mo-ther come up with a plan,
Mir-iam and her bro-ther crossed the de-sert sand,
Oh, the way to free-dom can be ve-ry long.

saved young bro-ther Mo-ses
Lea-ding all the peo-ple
When they got dis-cou-raged,

from old pha-raoh's hand. Mir-iam, shake your tam-bou-rine.
to the pro-mised land. Mir-iam, shake your tam-bou-rine.
Mir-iam sang her song. Mir-iam, shake your tam-bou-rine.

Mir-iam, shake your tam-bou-rine and dance for the love of God.
Mir-iam, shake your tam-bou-rine and dance for the love of God.
Mir-iam, shake your tam-bou-rine and dance for the love of God.

Words & Music ©1992 Sally Browder
Arr. ©1992 Luther Mitchell, Jr.

SONGS OF JOY — 141

OUR GOD IS A SHE AND A HE

Our God is a Mother and a Father too, Our God is the Friend who will always pull us through. Our God is a Sister who loves you and me. And God is a Brother who sets us free. Our God is a

Words ©1992 Jann Aldredge-Clanton

Arr. ©1992 Luther Mitchell, Jr.
19th Century Shaker tune

142 　　　　　　　　　　　　　　　　　　　　　　　SONGS OF JOY

She and a He, But Loving God is much more you see. For a God who could make both you and me, Is as great as great can be.

SONGS OF JOY _____ 143

GOD IS LIKE NO OTHER

God is like my mo-ther, God is like my fa-ther, God is like no o-ther For God is God of all. God is like my bro-ther, God is like my sis-ter. You too will dis-co-ver that God is God of all.

Words©1992 Jann Aldredge-Clanton & L. Mitchell   Music©1992 Luther Mitchell, Jr.

DEBORAH'S SONG

Deborah led her people, Spoke God's Word to them, Showed them all the right way, When their eyes grew dim. Sing a song of gladness, For God's loving care. Let us sing like Deborah God's great love to share. Awake, awake, Deborah! Awake and sing a song!

Words ©1992 Jann Aldredge-Clanton

Music ©1992 Luther Mitchell, Jr.

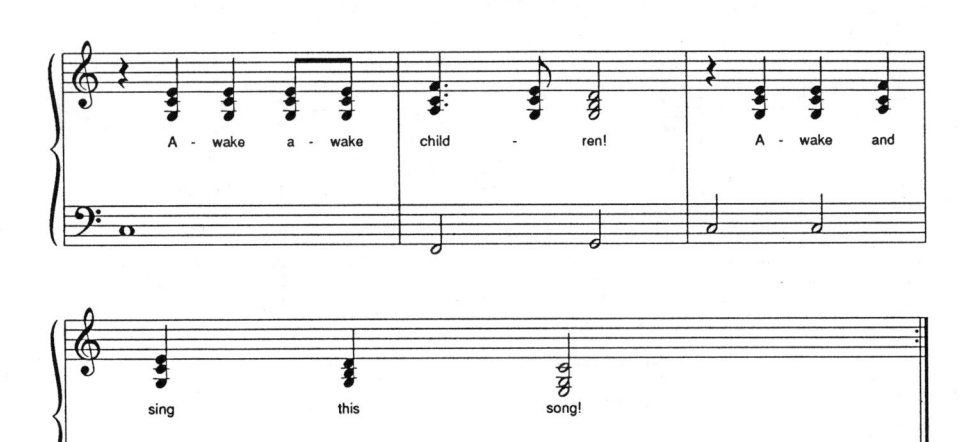

SONGS OF JOY — 145

ALL CHILDREN TOGETHER

God made all chil-dren on this big earth; black,
yel-low, red, brown, and white. God brings bright flo-wers and
trees to birth, And sun, moon, and stars to light.

God is the Friend who is al-ways there, Who
hears us when we are sad. This Friend we know will
al-ways care, And make us a-gain feel glad.

WORDS ©1992 Jann Aldredge-Clanton

Tune O HOW I LOVE JESUS
Anonymous, 19th Century

SONGS OF JOY — 147

All chil-dren to-ge-ther, All chil-dren to-ge-ther, All chil-dren to-ge-ther, Sing prai-ses to God, our Friend.

I AM SO GLAD

I am so glad that God loves us so much, Gave us a world full of
beauty to touch. Wonderful things all around us we see,
Showing how dearly God loves you and me.
I am so glad God loves you and me, loves you and me, loves you and me.

Flowers and sunshine spread beauty around,
Laughter and friendship surround us each day.
Showing us clearly God's love is the way.

Words ©1992 Jann Aldredge-Clanton

Tune JESUS LOVES EVEN ME
Philip P. Bliss, 1838-1876

SONGS OF JOY — 149

Refrain

I am so glad God loves you and me. God loves us all so much.

THERE IS ROOM IN MY HEART

You did leave your throne and your heav'n ly crown, When you came here to earth for
The— whole world rang when the an - gels sang, Pro— claim ing to all peace on

me; But in Beth - le - hem's home was there found no room For your ho - ly na - ti - vi -
earth; But no place was found but the cold, hard ground In a sta - ble your low - ly

Refrain
ty. O come to my heart, Christ Je - sus, There is room in my heart for you.
birth.

Words Emily E. S. Elliott, 1836-1897
Adapt.©1992 Jann Aldredge-Clanton

Tune MARGARET
Timothy R. Matthews, 1826-1910

SONGS OF JOY — 151

PRAISE GOD, ALL YOU LITTLE CHILDREN

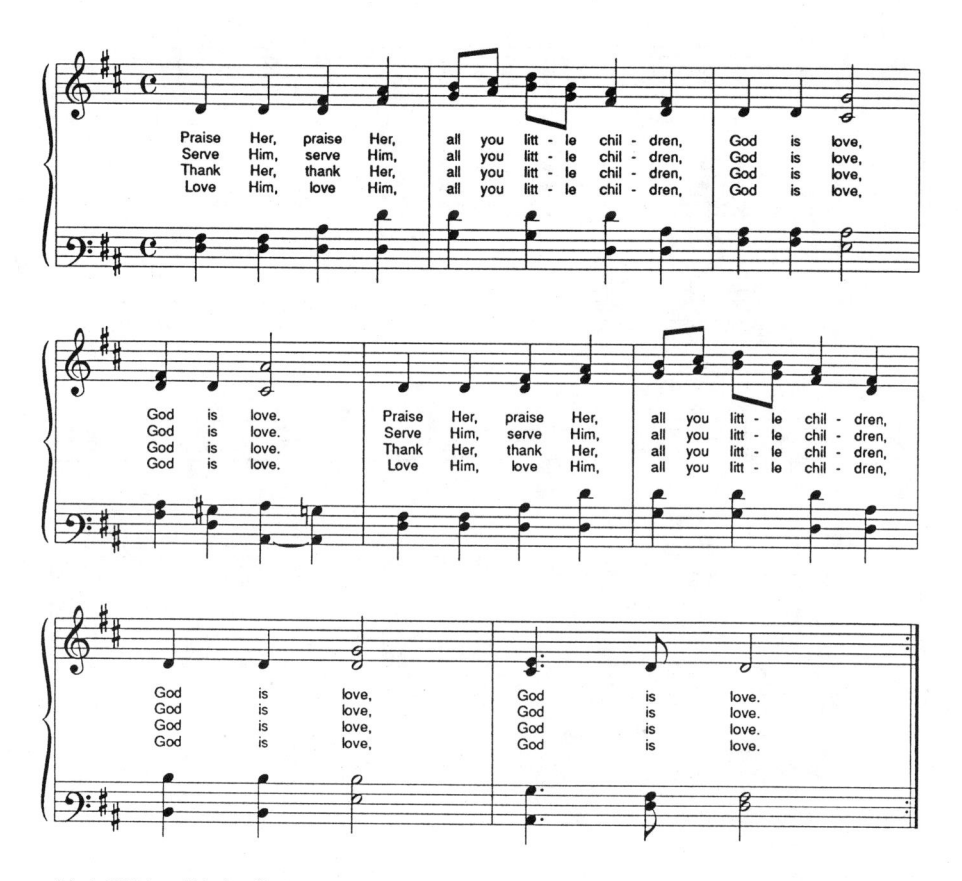

Praise Her, praise Her, all you litt-le chil-dren, God is love,
Serve Him, serve Him, all you litt-le chil-dren, God is love,
Thank Her, thank Her, all you litt-le chil-dren, God is love,
Love Him, love Him, all you litt-le chil-dren, God is love.

God is love. Praise Her, praise Her, all you litt-le chil-dren,
God is love. Serve Him, serve Him, all you litt-le chil-dren,
God is love. Thank Her, thank Her, all you litt-le chil-dren,
God is love. Love Him, love Him, all you litt-le chil-dren,

God is love, God is love.
God is love, God is love.
God is love, God is love.
God is love, God is love.

Adapt. 1992 Jann Aldredge-Clanton

Anonymous

Tune GOD IS LOVE

Anonymous

152   SONGS OF JOY

INTO MY HEART

In - to my heart, in - to my heart, Come in - to my heart, Christ Je - sus. Come in to - day, come in to stay. Come in - to my heart, Christ Je - sus.

Words & Music ©1924 Harry D. Clarke

Renewal 1952 by Hope Publishing Co, Carol Stream, IL 60188. All rights reserved. Used by permission.

Words adapt. 1992 Jann Aldredge-Clanton

SONGS OF JOY — 153

GOD'S BEAUTIFUL WORLD

God's beau-ti-ful world, God's beau-ti-ful world, I love God's beau-ti-ful world. She made it for you, He made it for me, I love God's beau-ti-ful world.

Words Aurora M. Shumate

Music Ida T. Truss ©1939:

Renewal 1967 Broadman Press.

All rights reserved. Used by permission.

Adapt. 1992 Jann Aldredge-Clanton

DEEP AND WIDE

Words & Music Herbert G. Tovey, 1946

SONGS OF JOY 155

CLIMB SUNSHINE MOUNTAIN

Climb, climb up sunshine mountain, Heav'nly breezes blow;
Climb, climb up sunshine mountain, Faces all aglow. Turn, turn from sin and doubting, Look to God on high; Climb, climb up sunshine mountain You and I.

Words and music Harry Dixon Loes. Copyright © 1944 Singspiration Music/ASCAP.

All rights reserved. Used by permission of Benson Music Group, Inc.

WONDER SONG

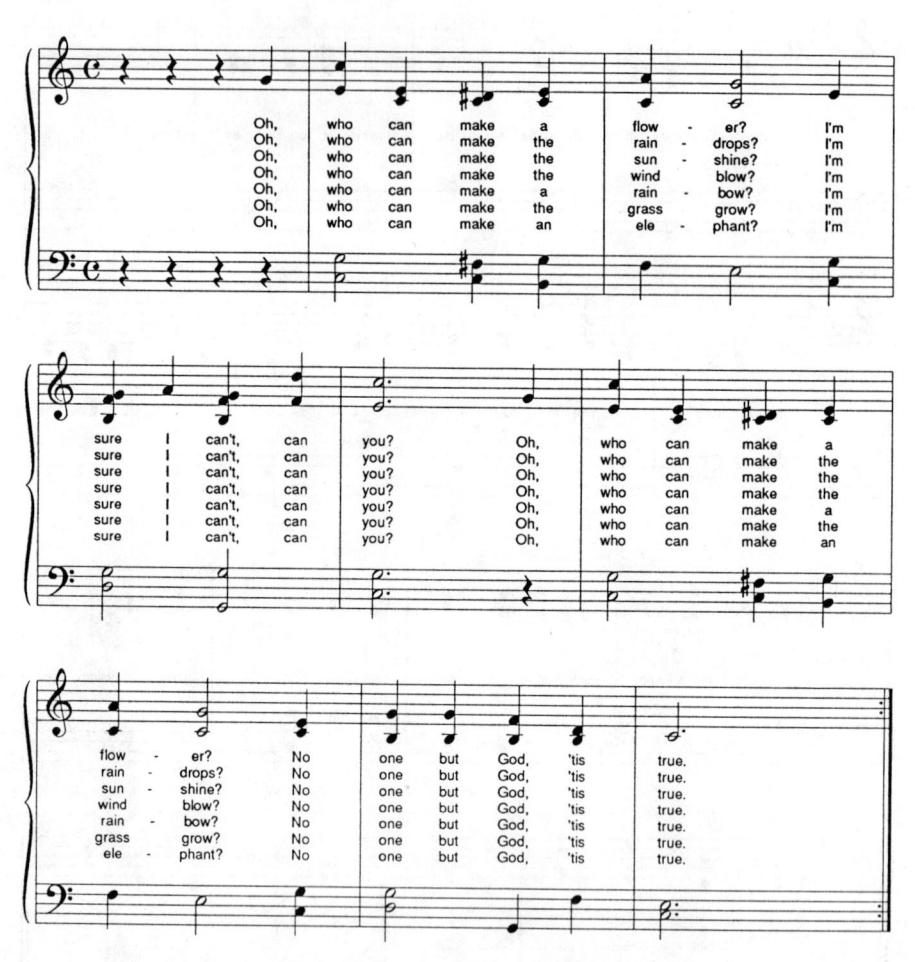

Oh, who can make a flower? I'm sure I can't, can you? Oh, who can make a flower? No one but God, 'tis true.
Oh, who can make the raindrops? I'm sure I can't, can you? Oh, who can make the raindrops? No one but God, 'tis true.
Oh, who can make the sunshine? I'm sure I can't, can you? Oh, who can make the sunshine? No one but God, 'tis true.
Oh, who can make the wind blow? I'm sure I can't, can you? Oh, who can make the wind blow? No one but God, 'tis true.
Oh, who can make a rainbow? I'm sure I can't, can you? Oh, who can make a rainbow? No one but God, 'tis true.
Oh, who can make the grass grow? I'm sure I can't, can you? Oh, who can make the grass grow? No one but God, 'tis true.
Oh, who can make an elephant? I'm sure I can't, can you? Oh, who can make an elephant? No one but God, 'tis true.

Ask children to add things God made.

Words Grace W. Owens
Adapt. 1992 Jann Aldredge-Clanton

Music Clara Lee Parker

NOTES

INTRODUCTION

1. *Children's Letters to God*, compiled by Eric Marshall and Stuart Hample (New York: Simon and Schuster, 1966), n.p.
2. Martin Luther King, Jr., *Where Do We Go from Here: Chaos or Community?* (New York: Harper & Row, 1967), 41.
3. Robert S. Siegler in *Children's Thinking* (Englewood Cliffs, N.J.: Prentice-Hall, 1986), 40–41, discusses this theory of development made famous by Piaget.
4. John Flavell, "Really and Truly," *Psychology Today* 20 (January 1986): 44.
5. Alison Gopnik and Janet W. Astington, "Children's Understanding of Representational Change and Its Relation to the Understanding of False Belief and the Appearance-Reality Distinction," *Child Development* 59 (February 1988): 34.
6. David Heller, "The Children's God," *Psychology Today* 19 (December 1985): 25.
7. David Heller, *The Children's God* (Chicago: University of Chicago Press, 1986), 57–71.
8. Anne Agee and Gary Kline, *The Basic Writer's Book*, 2d ed. (Englewood Cliffs, N.J.: Prentice-Hall, 1981), 123.

GETTING STARTED

9. For inclusive-language biblical translations, use the New Revised Standard Version and change the masculine words for God to non-gender words, or alternate masculine and feminine words.
10. Jerome W. Berryman, "Being in Parables with Children," *Religious Education* 74, no. 3 (May–June 1979): 280–81. For this activity and others I am influenced by Berryman's work in the religious education of children based on Maria Montessori's approach.

APPENDIX: INCLUSIVE-LANGUAGE RESOURCES FOR ADULTS

Carlisle, Thomas John. *Eve and After: Old Testament Women in Portrait.* Grand Rapids: Eerdmans, 1984.
———. *Beginning with Mary: Women of the Gospels in Portrait.* Grand Rapids: Eerdmans, 1986.
Clanton, Jann Aldredge. *In Whose Image? God and Gender.* New York: Crossroad, 1990.
Duck, Ruth C., ed. *Bread for the Journey: Resources for Worship.* New York: Pilgrim Press, 1981.
Duck, Ruth C., and Michael G. Brausch. *Everflowing Streams: Songs for Worship.* New York: Pilgrim Press, 1981.
Emswiler, Sharon Neufer, and Thomas Neufer Emswiler, eds. *Sisters and Brothers Sing!* 2d ed. Normal, Ill.: Wesley Foundation, 1977.
———. *Wholeness in Worship: Creative Models for Sunday, Family, and Special Services.* San Francisco: Harper & Row, 1980.
———. *Women and Worship.* San Francisco: Harper & Row, 1974.
Hardesty, Nancy A. *Inclusive Language in the Church.* Atlanta: John Knox Press, 1987.
Huber, Jane Parker. *Joy in Singing.* Atlanta: Office of Women and Joint Office of Worship of the Presbyterian Church, 1983.
———. *A Singing Faith.* Philadelphia: Westminster, 1987.
An Inclusive Language Lectionary. Division of Education and Ministry, National Council of Churches of Christ in the U.S.A. Published for the Cooperative Publication Association by John Knox Press, Atlanta; Pilgrim Press, New York; Westminster Press, Philadelphia; 1983.
Miller, Casey, and Kate Swift. *The Handbook of Nonsexist Writing.* New York: Lippincott and Crowell, 1980.
Mitchell, Rosemary Catalano, and Gail Anderson Ricciuti. *Birthings and Blessings: Liberating Worship Services for the Inclusive Church.* New York: Crossroad, 1991.

Presbyterian Hymnal. Louisville, Ky.: Westminster/John Knox Press, 1990. Includes new hymns using inclusive language and changes some traditional hymns to make language referring to humanity inclusive.

Psalms Anew: In Inclusive Language. Trans. Nancy Schreck and Maureen Leach. Winona, Minn.: Saint Mary's Press, 1986.

Ruether, Rosemary Radford. *Sexism and God-Talk: Toward a Feminist Theology.* Boston: Beacon Press, 1983.

———. *Women-Church: Theology and Practice.* San Francisco: Harper & Row, 1986.

———. *Womanguides: Readings Toward a Feminist Theology.* Boston: Beacon Press, 1985.

Russell, Letty, M. ed. *The Liberating Word: A Guide to Non-Sexist Interpretation of the Bible.* Philadelphia: Westminster, 1976.

Schaffran, Janet, and Pat Kozak. *More Than Words: Prayer and Ritual for Inclusive Communities.* Bloomington, Ind.: Meyer-Stone Books, 1986.

The United Methodist Hymnal. Nashville: United Methodist Publishing House, 1988. Includes new hymns with inclusive images of God and changes some traditional hymns to make language inclusive.

Watkins, Keith. *Faithful and Fair: Transcending Sexist Language in Worship.* Nashville: Abingdon, 1981.

Winter, Miriam Therese. *WomanPrayer, WomanSong.* Bloomington, Ind.: Meyer-Stone Books, 1987.

———. *WomanWisdom.* New York: Crossroad, 1991.

———. *WomanWitness.* New York: Crossroad, 1992.

———. *WomanWord.* New York: Crossroad, 1990.

Words That Hurt and Words That Heal: Language about God and People. Nashville: United Methodist Publishing House, 1985.

Wren, Brian. *What Language Shall I Borrow?* New York: Crossroad, 1990.